Rent (minus) Control

Bulletproof

R.B. Winters

DEDICATION

This book is for the friends who have stuck by me while the world changed.

And for Mom.

Table of Contents

Rent (minus) Control: Bulletproof

Preface

By the time you reach the end of this book you may wonder why I would write it in the first place. This is my first official work of non-fiction. The two books leading us to this point are a mixture of fact and fiction, and to avoid bruising egos or dealing with angry "characters" I labeled them both as fiction.

This book, however, has a very different purpose. The intent, as always, is to engage you as the reader, but it was actually a more selfish motive driving me to pour words across the page. You see, when my mother passed away unexpectedly, the following days and weeks were a mess of people trying to pry information out of me. At the time I wasn't comfortable giving away the intimate details. But I've had a change of heart. Being the marketing-minded person I am, and also wanting to ensure the truth was known, this book outlines everything that happened from the beginning to the end of the event.

To satisfy my own ego, I will assume you have read the previous iterations of 'Rent (minus) Control.' This means you have some awareness to the close relationship between my mother and I. Our relationship was so much more than a typical mother-son situation, and I think to understand how I got here, to this book, you have to understand how I arrived here at this place.

At the age of twenty-two, I loaded up my Honda Element and declared I was moving to New York. I'd moved out at seventeen and bounced around from Vegas to Baltimore, but none of those places fit. It was always supposed to be New York, and these more affordable cities were like torture trying to get myself the desired end goal. The day I left there was one-hundred and eighty dollars in my bank account. Of course, Mom asked me if I had money and if I would be okay. Being twenty-two and really having no clue what I was doing I confirmed being fine. Knowing the reality, she emptied all of the money from her purse into my hand. It was somewhere around three-hundred dollars.

In a miraculous twist of fate, I managed to survive in New York. One year, two, three and so on to the point where I'm nearing the big ten. The distance never impacted the relationship between Mom and myself. If anything, it became stronger and we grew into great friends. We spoke every day, and we spoke about everything. My "dates," her relationships, and so on. That was the area where we were the same and completely different.

My mother was the strongest person I've ever known. She came from nothing and made herself a life that was self-sufficient. There was one thing she had which I saw as a weakness. She had an enormous heart. She would give you the shirt off of her back, that's the positive, but the negative is that she desired the "great love" so many people want.

I watched from an early age as she, actually as both of my parents, struggled to find a lasting love. I've seen more bad marriages, break-ups, meltdowns and cop calling than most people see in a marathon of watching court television. As far back as I can recall I told myself to never behave this way. To survive dating I've very successfully built an armor to keep out any threat of love. Which was an interesting part of building this story, because my ability to turn off emotion and only act on logic came into play in such unexpected ways.

This is not to say I'm cold or empty. I love my family and my friends, those are the people I allow past the armor and they get to know the real person. Which may sound odd as friends can hurt you, but I have enough trust in the people around me to not suffer from such fear.

Mom said it best one night after a few beers when she gave me a call. She was listening to the Fleetwood Mac song, Thrown Down. She called to tell me there was a line: *You're not like other people, you do what you want to.* She called to tell me that line was me and why she was so proud of me. I will always remember that as it made a big impact. Actually, there are many things she said which I'm grateful to have heard because my brother and sister did not have the same luxury.

So, why write this book? I mean, other than to capitalize on woe. Mom was the biggest fan of anything I wrote and also my best PR person. She probably would have argued with the storyline, but just as she urged me to do with the last book, which unfortunately came out right after her passing, be extreme, offensive and inappropriate. That's what gets book sales.

I'm taking her advice and at the same time giving people all the information they were begging to have.

Rent (minus) Control: Bulletproof

1. Calls

On this particularly warm March morning I was feeling a bit off. Almost as if I was depressed, but having no reason to be feeling in such a mood. In an attempt to shake the feeling from my mind and take in a little fresh air, that being the smell of car exhaust and ominous trash odors of New York, a walk around the new neighborhood seemed to be the best idea.

My building on the Upper East Side had recently made the decision to replace the feisty building manager. In place of a strict screening process which took personality into account as much as credit scores, it was evident anyone could now move into the building. From my corner of the hallway, a man moved in to the right. He was a pothead who enjoyed all forms of smoking, as it smelled, about anything he could wrap his lips around was going up in puffs of smoke. To my left came a woman who cried, without fail, on a nightly basis. At first, I was curious if perhaps she was being smacked around by an angry boyfriend or jealous lover, disgruntled by her infidelity or possibly just easily enraged.

Rent (minus) Control: Bulletproof

Listening intently with my ear pressed against the wall on more than a few occasions, I would try to capture any sound of scuffling or a swift slap, but nothing. There was definitely a television playing in the background. Quite possibly the source driving my neighbor to tears. Perhaps in place of an abusive relationship she emotionally sliced her soul with sad movies.

Then there was the worst of all the new neighbors: A stomper living directly above my head. Ignoring the problem for weeks, steps belted down over me from six in the morning until just after midnight every-single-day. It must be another writer or artist of some sort living up there, I thought, because they were home more than I was, which is really saying something. Finally reaching my limit, I walked up the stairs, knocked on the door and prepared to share my complaint with whomever was holding up inside. Until the door opened. Mouth gaping, the tenant living above me was a tiny, little Asian girl. She was barely five feet tall and maybe one-hundred pounds on her worst day. Was it possible all the noise was coming from this miniature Godzilla monster? No, it couldn't be possible. I excused myself, feeling slightly embarrassed at what had to be an overreaction, only to return to my apartment minutes later and discover she was, without a doubt, the evil noise maker.

Having one bad neighbor is stressful, but three was painful to the point of needing medication to tolerate the stress. Writing became nearly impossible as I was putting a great amount of effort into finding ways to occupy time outside of the apartment. Running in the park, meeting my friend Dimitri for coffee on his lunch break and a number of other activities. None of these would have been even half enjoyable if my laptop were to tag along. Meaning the laptop sat sleeping at home while I traipsed around and accomplished nothing. When the renewal papers for my lease arrived I was quick to decline and begin the apartment hunt.

Finding the perfect apartment in Manhattan is impossible unless you have a hefty six figure salary and an enormous down payment collecting annual interest pennies in a savings account. As an indie author completing freelance copywriting work to pay the bills, I was in no position to buy an apartment...probably not even a cardboard box by New York standards. Renting remains the only option.

It took thirty-six apartment viewings and two brokers before I came across an apartment to call home. Not to mention a battle with the first broker to return his fee after he tried pulling a bait and switch. Originally, apartment number twenty-two was the one I committed to renting. The application was complete, deposit check made out and everything signed, sealed and delivered. Or, so I thought. Two days later the landlord didn't have the unit I had viewed available, but a similar unit in the same building. Not trying to be totally unreasonable, I viewed the alternate apartment. Half the size, double the grime and a ten-fold increase on the depression anyone living there would experience. That was a deal breaker. To my surprise the broker was extremely willing to terminate services. I must truly be a terrible person to assist in the apartment hunting process.

Getting the deposit back was the real problem. Suddenly the broker was unreachable. Text messages and phone calls going unanswered left me with one option: Call his boss. Which is exactly what I did. Within an hour of my call I had three different men blowing up my phone with different reasons for why I couldn't have the deposit back. Not in the mood to play the Jewish landlord game I'd left behind in Brooklyn, I had a friend make a call and pretend to be my lawyer. The next call I received was to inform me the deposit would be available at the broker's Midtown office in an hour. The power of lawyer...well, the power of liars.

The second broker was a quirky lady who made me think of someone who in twenty years will be living in her apartment with two dozen cats. Based on the amount of fur stuck to her purple peacoat each time we met, it's possible this scenario is already playing out in her life. But she had a friendly demeanor, really understood my desire to not move so far from my current apartment that I lost the benefits of the area: Clean streets, an older demographic, no loud music or parties.

And then we found the one. A one-bedroom on Sixty-Second Street. Depending on who you ask this is Midtown East. Others would say Upper East Side because we're above Fifty-Ninth Street. I go with the latter because the Upper East Side has a certain clout I find appealing. Also, who the hell wants to live in Midtown?

Now, somewhere between Midtown and the Upper East Side, I'm strolling along under a gray sky. The winter had been a long and heavy burden, and though March is only beginning this one day of semi-warmth is enough to give hope winter may soon come to a close.

The first stop on my walk is of course, Starbucks. Conveniently only a block away, though this isn't such a surprise as Starbucks is only a block away from everything in Manhattan.

Next to the coffee shop is Bed, Bath & Beyond, offering amazing deals and making it easier than ever for me to splurge on the apartment furnishings I don't really need but can't live without owning. The two retailers consume an entire length of city block, metal chairs forming a pavilion in front of both. What neither building planners accounted for when adding seating was the homeless population. Every day I see a different selection of rough looking men and sometimes women passed out in the uncomfortable wiry chairs, all their belongings stacked in bags beside them, pigeons lurking at their feet for crumbs. At any moment they looked ready to spring to life and attack.

This Starbucks wasn't completely new to me, having been here a handful of times before, and from the first visit I was having issues with the gay barista. It was hard to say what his problem with me was exactly, as it only seemed to be with me. For example, he would politely help whomever was before or after me, but when it was my turn to order he would stare grumpily without saying a word. I'd provide my order and sometimes he'd 'forget' to call it out and I'd end up having to tell the other barista who was working the expresso machine. But no matter, he was a cranky gay and there's nothing I can do other than grin and get on with life. Though this delicious vanilla latte makes me give two less shits about him.

Being in this funk it only seemed appropriate to call Mom. I'd missed her call the night before while at my friend, Dimitri's, house in Astoria for dinner. Too drunk and heading home too late I didn't return the call before heading off to bed. Which is a generous description. After falling up the new building's many marble stairs several times, plunging through the creaky apartment door and onto the plush couch, I passed out, face down with glasses on in a rather uncomfortable position. Come to think of it, perhaps the sensation I'm feeling isn't depression, maybe it's a hangover from four bottles of shared wine.

Either way, Mom was sure to have drama to distract my spinning mind. She had begun dating a Latino some weeks back, her first non-white guy and as she put it, 'He has the biggest dick ever.' To me this was a win-win. She was diversifying her contacts and getting a decent piece of meat. This new guy was a tad temperamental and prone to picking fights as I understood. Friday night, while organizing the new apartment, we gabbed on the phone for a few hours about what an asshole the guy is and how, 'If he wasn't good in bed, she'd be out the door.'

Dialing the phone it rang several times before going to voicemail. She must have ended up at the boyfriend's house for the weekend. It had become common for her to not pick up the phone around her boyfriend. Even though I'm her son he had an issue with her talking to other men...even if they are related by blood. In my mind he's a psycho, but who am I to stand in the way of a good sexual encounter.

Unable to ease my mind with a stroll, I eventually found myself back home. The sofa called to me...*watch bad television and eat things you'll want to throw-up later.* It's terrible when a piece of furniture knows me so well. And that's exactly how I spent the better part of the day. What a bust. No friends to play with and no one to talk to on the phone...even though I generally despise phone calls. Just this once I'm feeling the itch to chat.

Being Sunday, as it is, at some point I must do homework. Grad school was treating me well. It was like Kindergarten for adults. The assignments were all about interpretation and opinion, things I love and was always criticized for during my undergraduate work. Giving in to my mental anguish, I logged on to the computer and looked up the week's assignments.

Create Project: Spell the word 'ART' using personal objects.

Are you kidding me? This is two minutes of work for twenty points. Like so many of the other projects, this wasn't stretching my mind to the limits of thinking, but it was allowing creativity to play a role in education. Pulling a few thin framed photos from the wall I created an 'A.' The photos were many of the friends I left behind in moving to New York, one of my sister and her kids and even my long deceased Pug, Chico. To create the 'R' I pulled out leftover copies of my last two books. And where would any of us be without money? For the 'T' dollars formed the shape. Only appropriate as I'm broke and dollars are the only cash at hand.

Maneuvering to take a photo of the objects spread across the hardwood floor without capturing my shadow the phone rang. Interrupting the photo, I glanced at the screen, a 435 area code. It was definitely someone from Utah, but anyone calling after eight was no one I wanted to hear from and likely to be some aggressive bill collector. Ignoring the call I opened the camera app once more, snapping the photo. It turned out pretty good, though part of my head's shadow was cast over the bottom of the 'T.' We'll call it artistic flair.

As I uploaded the photo to the class bulletin board the phone rang once more. Before seeing the screen I was annoyed with the relentless stranger. What about voicemail didn't give you the impression your call is unwelcome? Eyes on the screen, this time the Caller ID read: Dad. That's weird, he almost never calls me, and at eight-thirty, he must have something important to say. A lump formed in my throat, it was probably about my grandma. Maybe she died and he was calling to break the bad news.

"Hello."

"Hey, B, how are you?" My parents never recognized my choice to change my name from Brian to Ryan and drop the use of our last name. For them I would always be, 'B.'

"I'm fine. How are you?" Dad had a weird sound in his voice. Something like when he told me, Frisky, my cat was dead as a child. In a twist to the story, years later I would find out my stepmother at the time put the cat to sleep. Man, she was such a bitch.

"Are you sitting down?" he asked, the tone not wavering, but remaining steadfast and uncomfortable.

Now I was worried. Bad news was absolutely coming. It had to be about grandma, she'd been sick for as long as I can remember. Age ninety is an accomplishment, but I was always surprised by her ailments. You've never met someone so faithful to their religion and so obviously ignored, or possibly tested, by their God.

"Yes. Why?"

"It's your mom."

"What about her?" I asked, my heart skipping a beat as his voice choked back tears. Watch him tell me she's been arrested for something.

"She passed away."

2. Cry

Nearly an hour passed before I was able to compose and pick myself up from the floor. In a moment, which I'm certain will remain in my mind as long as I live, the news of my mother's death was so unexpected that my legs became unable to support my body. Rushing toward the bathroom for a tissue as tears flooded over my face and sobs lurched from my mouth, air doing its best to get in and keep me conscious, I made it as far as two steps from the couch.

The details weren't enough to sustain a mind that plays the 'why' game during every waking moment. Terminal lung cancer. This was the cause provided to me. I told her a thousand times to stop smoking, going so far as to call a quit smoking line for her and have nicotine patches mailed. Now all I could wonder was which cigarette was the one. Which cigarette, which puff of smoke, was the one to set off a chain of events bringing us to a moment in time where everything has stopped?

My mind was attempting to wrap around the concept at hand, I needed to let my boss know the stack of copywriting he'd requested wouldn't be coming any time soon. I sent a concise text message, mainly because words are difficult to form through grumbling sobs, *'My mom died. I'll need some time off.'* Moments later the phone rang.

"He-hello?" Pull it together as best I could to speak.
"Are you ok?" Dennis asked.

Dennis was the person signing off on my paychecks for brief copywriting assignments, but I'd known him for years and we'd become good friends. It is for this reason I answered the phone instead of letting it ring endlessly.

"I don't know what I am."
"Is there anything I can do?"
"No."
"Do you want me to come up?"

Dennis lived out of state, the offer was incredibly generous but not necessary. I meant it when I said I didn't know what I was, and that extended to needs. What do you need in a moment of personal crisis? Solitude was probably the best option.

"No, I'll be fine," I lied.
"Have you told anyone?"
"I'm not ready for my friends to see me cry."
"I'm going to come up."

It was getting late, but the energy needed to be strong and refuse someone's offer to let me cry on their shoulder was too much effort.

"Okay."

After ending the call I thought about texting Dimitri or Larry. I had the urge to share this news, but it seemed unfair to drag others into sadness they didn't cause nor have a tie to. If I should text anyone, it should be the Animator, he knew Mom and she loved him, but he has enough drama in his life without this to add stress. With no clear options, I would need to keep the information to myself.

This feels unreal, impossible even. But if you tell someone your personal news, it then becomes fact. Fact was the one thing I wasn't ready to deal with. The one thing I was ready to deal with was the bottle of wine I'd opened moments before Dad called. With my eyes taking a temporary break from dripping wildly, it was an opportunity to begin consuming the liquid numbing agent.

The additional adrenaline rushing through my veins neutralized the bottle of wine as fast as each gulp could get inside. Of course, there wasn't another drop of alcohol in the apartment the one time it was necessary. Dawning a paperboy cap, pulled down as far over my eyes as was possible, I put on a jacket and walked to the Duane Reade around the corner.

"We're closing," said the Indian manager.

Ignoring him as I entered, rushing the icebox along the wall, pulling out a twelve-pack of beer. Placing it on the counter to pay, the Indian man caught a glimpse of my face. I felt puffy and holding back tears wasn't helping, but I must look like real shit to get that facial reaction. He didn't even ask for my ID, amazing as this location always asked for ID from everyone. Beer in hand, I headed back to the apartment.

I'd had at least six or seven more drinks before Dennis rang the buzzer. As I let him into the apartment I thought how odd it was I didn't feel even the slightest buzz from the alcohol; clearly numbing myself was not going to work.

"How are you doing?" Dennis asked, trying to be sympathetic, but knowing I was likely to be emotionally explosive.

"I feel like shit."

"You look pretty rough."

"Yeah, I figured when the guy at the corner store gave me sad face."

"Is there anything open nearby? We could go grab a drink and talk."

"Baker Street, a pub up the street might still be open."

We made it just in time for last call. The bartender seeing my red, tear-lined face, providing us each two beers as he finished watching the game with some random drunk in the corner.

"So, what happened?"

"My dad said she had lung cancer." Now it was real. I could feel the tears bubbling up again, the lump in my throat forming as I tried to force my emotions back inside.

"Did she know?" Dennis asked, the same thing I'd asked my dad.

"He told me she had called him the night before, incredibly drunk, telling him she had it but that he couldn't tell me."

"So, no one knew?"

"I guess not. But that's not the worst part."

"What do you mean?"

"She called and told him yesterday. That was her goodbye call. He said she called him around seven. She called me a little after eight but I didn't answer. I was at Dimitri's in Astoria having fun and muted my phone. I missed my goodbye call."

"You can't think like that," Dennis urged.

"But I do."

"She wouldn't want you to think that way and beat yourself up."

"I know I'm not supposed to think this," I spat sarcastically. "But it's me after all."

"What's your plan?"

"I guess I need to book a plane ticket and fly to Utah in the morning. You know what the really crazy thing is?"

"What's that?"

"I've been creating a timeline in my head. She must have found out she was sick about six months ago."

"How do you figure?" Dennis asked, sipping at his beer.

"That's when she started giving me hypothetical situations. Like, *'If I were to die'* do this and that. I didn't think much of it at the time, I thought she was just being morbid, we always talked about random things all the time."

"It probably doesn't help for me to say this, but at least she told you what she wants."

"Yeah, you're right. She was very clear with what I should do. I'm to cremate her and spread the ashes."

Allowing the word 'cremate' to enter the conversation gave me another jolt of reality, the tears once more welling up. A strong case of the 'why's' followed. Why did this happen? Why didn't she tell me she was sick?

"How old was your Mom?"

"Only fifty-two, she's too young to die," I rationalized. "I think I should go home, take a big sleeping pill and try to sleep."

"Do you want me to help with anything?"

"Can you help me find a flight out tomorrow morning?"

"Sure, whatever you need."

"Are you staying at a hotel? You're welcome to stay at my place and I'll sleep on the sofa." It was the least I could do considering Dennis had come into the city just to hear me whine.

"I booked a room around the corner. I'll text you some flight times and we can figure it out in the morning."

"Okay. Thank you, I really appreciate it."

Rent (minus) Control: Bulletproof

We exited the bar and Dennis hailed a cab to take him towards Lexington Avenue. I walked the two blocks home, the streets void of life, my tears going unheard.

3. Newark

A long, sleepless night left me feeling exhausted. The silver lining; Dennis booked us both airline tickets the evening before when he returned to the hotel. What I was trying to understand was why he selected Newark International as the point of departure. This meant we needed to either hop a train or bus and make the hike all the way across the Hudson.

Bless the individual that invented sunglasses. A large pair of black Ray-Bans assisted in concealing my face. Arriving at the Starbucks on Lexington Avenue across from Dennis' hotel I ordered a coffee.

"Can I get a grande vanilla latte, please?" Wow, was the scratchy, grumble my voice?

The barista gave me eyes, writing my order on a cup and handing it off to another guy for brewing. She probably thought my voice was worn from a night of drinking and drugging. I'd had plenty to drink the night before, but the voice was an unexpected side effect of heaving and sobbing. I feel disgusting and pathetic.

Collecting my drink, I made the short walk to Hotel 57. A plush Renaissance Hotel I'd had a drink in on more than one occasion. It didn't surprise me Dennis selected this place on short notice. They were known for kissing ass and all but giving customers hand jobs to ensure satisfaction.

The door opened to reveal a bellhop. He greeted me, searching with his eyes for baggage; it was there, there's just no way to see it unless my mouth opens. A brief smile and I schlepped up a spiral marble staircase to the restaurant reserved for elite guests. Dennis waved me in, the female attendant smiling broadly as she pulled back the massive glass pane.

"Feeling any better?" Dennis asked, a newspaper and an iced tea on the circular table between us.

"No, but I'll lie and say yes if you'd prefer." I may feel like crap, but my sense of humor is still intact. *Thank god.*

"We have about an hour before we need to leave for the airport. Do you want anything to eat?"

"I'm not hungry. How are we getting to the airport?"

"I have my car."

"You're just going to leave your car at the airport? In Jersey."

"They have long term parking." Dennis gave me a glare, this was an obvious answer.

"Right."

We conversed while Dennis finished off his tea, my mind having difficulty staying on point. If I didn't put effort into concentrating on the words coming at me it felt as if I might doze off. This left Dennis to hold up most of the conversation, there just wasn't anything worth saying.

A short while later, with breakfast finished and his bag packed, we retrieved a BMW SUV from the hotel garage. Stopping by my apartment to grab a bag full of clothing and assorted bathroom items we were on our way. Seeing as I'm a Virgo and we have less than three hours before the flight is scheduled to depart, panic and stress are setting in.

Rather than listen to my directions, Dennis allowed the GPS to guide us. I may not be an above ground expert, considering I never drive, but I walk all over Manhattan. The demon GPS, in an effort to torment me further, led us through clogged streets and backed up avenues in the direction of the Holland Tunnel. Biting back my complaints, I let my eyes wander as the buildings passed by the window. Each with a different color brick facade with a story I'd probably never know. People living inside each walk-up with their own lives and problems.

A short eternity later we pulled out of the tunnel, traffic speeding up as the expressway expanded on the Jersey side. I turned back to see the Manhattan skyline. An iconic skyline representing so much to so many, but for me it was a place where I'd made a million memories with my mother. Now, I choke back tears as the memories are ghostly and uncomfortable.

Rent (minus) Control: Bulletproof

Monday must not be a big travel day for Newark businessmen. The airport was mostly empty, even security couldn't slow us down with their ineffective procedures. With forty minutes to kill I located a restaurant with a bar. My appetite was kicking in for the first time today and if nothing else, I was in desperate need of a beer.

"Have you spoken to anyone in Utah?" Dennis asked, the bartender delivering our drinks.

"The funeral home called first thing this morning. She's in a town called Price, it's about an hour away from where she lived."

The gentleman from the funeral home had been exactly what you would expect. A mellow tone used to convey sympathy, even though I had to wonder if he even cared. After all, this is his job. The funeral man probably does this ten times a day.

"What about your siblings?"

"Not yet. I've spoken to a few family members that strong-armed the funeral home into giving them my cell. I figure once I'm off the plane I'll deal with them."

"If there's anything that you don't want to deal with just let me know. I'm happy to help."

"Thanks. I'm thinking I might need help at the funeral home. I don't want to see the body. I've never seen a dead person and that can't be my last memory of her."

"Would you like another beer?" asked the bartender, as I polished off the brown bottle.

Nodding my head fervently to signal an obvious 'yes.' Getting drunk now was my best chance for peace, the plane ride was five hours of pure boredom and overpriced drinks. Not to mention the likelihood of children. Screaming, crying, horrible little children. This is the number one thing you encounter on flights to Salt Lake City, baby capital of the world.

"Let me ask you, why Newark? JFK and LaGuardia are easier to reach from my apartment." I asked, the beer warm, but still drinkable.

"I figure this is a place you'll never want to go again, seemed like the better choice."

Sometimes people know you, and sometimes people *really* know you. I'd not made it nearly this far in my thinking, but Dennis was right, the likelihood I'd ever want to return to the airport where I flew home for this particular reason is one I'd rather not visit in the future.

Two more beers and I was feeling pretty good. Just in time for our flight to begin boarding. Stumbling into my seat, I pulled the shutter down. The last thing I wanted was for the Sun to illuminate my puffy face for the flight attendant. The usual plane takeoff process occurring and finally we were in the air and drinks came around. The fact they won't let you carry on a drink from the bar is a huge disappointment; mainly because my buzz was already beginning to wear off by the time a drink was back in hand. Idiotic tears seem to help things metabolize faster than normal. How I hate them.

When the Wi-Fi kicked in a message from Leo popped up on my phone's screen. I'd slipped out of his apartment a few months before, making the decision to stop seeing him. We weren't dating, but he caused me to be a mental case. That was until I realized having someone around with zero emotional interest is the best thing. It's the only way to have a functional fuck buddy relationship. *What are you up to tonight?*

Leo's timing is terrible, but on the other hand it's nice to know someone is thinking about you...even if it's only the naked version of you. *I'm planning a funeral. What about you?* Ok, probably too forward of me, but he asked. *Are you serious?* This is a fair question considering my sarcastic tendencies. *Yes. My mom died last night.* Sarcastic is one thing, but there's no energy in me at this moment to fluff someone.

Leo was sympathetic as anyone would be, but that instantly made me look at him as a human being. This meant our text-versation had to end. The only way I wanted to look at Leo was in the sexy, pants-free way. If at any moment you let your sex buddy in as anything more you're screwed. Metaphorically that is, they'll literally be fucking someone else.

Attempting to sleep proved a failure, instead I took this opportunity of semi-solitude to let my brain run wild. After all, I'm locked in a tube with no escape and it's probably as close to alone as I'll be for some time. My headphones played Stevie Nicks and Fleetwood Mac. It was only appropriate I let the music my parents introduced me to emotionally terrorize me. With my face pressed into the wall in an effort to conceal my very visible distress, the flight attendant stopped by before Dennis waved her away. She didn't know if I was about to go terrorist and pull out a bomb, or just self-destruct and leave her a mess to clean.

We eventually touched down in Salt Lake City. As we exited the plane I took a deep breath, swallowing any lingering emotions. Here we go.

4. Rachael

Long before New York, and way before I created my current persona, Robert Ryan, I was Brian. Earning my living by working retail as most people did during high school; some people even turning the art of fake smiles into a full blown career.

Having worked a few years for GAP in Park City, Utah, I was temporarily transferred to a Banana Republic store located conveniently behind the building. They were in need of a men's department manager and I was in need of a break from the women's department. No matter what any gay man tells you, every now and then you have to get away from the vagina, even if it's only temporary. But a short year later and I was back to the women's department and back to my old ways.

However, in retail a year is a long time and a staff can completely turnover. And did it. Gone were almost all of the familiar faces, other than the management staff. If you work in a small town and are able to claw your way to the top of a store's food chain, you better hold on for dear life. Because the moment you step away there are dozens of people willing to do more work for less money and you'll never be welcomed back into the fold. I was only lucky enough to have been on a temporary transfer, knowing there was a job to come back to.

The first night closing, I was folding a cube table of basic tee-shirts when a girl plopped down on the floor beside me. Covered in tattoos, many of them looking as old as my teenage self, she wasn't the type of person I would usually engage with unless forced. Seeing as this is work, I'm under forced pretenses. Rachael, the girl who was now sitting at my side, looked to be some sort of goth. Her hair was long and black, piercings on one side of her lip, heavy makeup on the eyes and lips.

Then she opened her mouth to speak. There are few people in the world that any of us instantly bond with, but when Rachael spoke it was clear the outside was a facade. Just as my preppy, outgoing personality was a facade for the store providing my paycheck. We were friends before the hour was up. The time between that moment and the day I announced I was moving to New York were filled with drunken weekends...and several drunken weekdays to be honest, and a million comical memories.

There was no one in the world other than Rachael, who I would ask to pick me up during a moment like this. She arrived to the airport late, as I expected of her. A bit more buzzed than anticipated, she climbed out of her car, knee high platforms laced to the top, a red and black corset and a black plaid miniskirt.

"Did you come from the bar?"

"Yes, but don't worry I stopped and got us a thirty-pack of PBR."

Some things you can grow out of, but white trash roots are something to be proud of, they add color to a boring world. Even if I do conceal them from my New York life.

"I love your planning skills."

"I knew the bar would be closed when you landed and we have to have a drink for Mom," Rachael explained.

Mom considered Rachael her daughter and often asked when we were getting married. Not in the straight, pressure sort of way. She wanted us to get married to ensure neither of us could ever get away from her.

"Dennis this is Rachael. Rachael, Dennis."

"Nice to meet you." Dennis extended a hand. Perhaps I should have provided him warning of how different Rachael and I are in appearance alone.

"Can we get something to eat?" I asked, still hungry from the meager snacks the airline provided between layovers.

Another thing I'd never grown out of was my love of diners. If it wasn't for fear of becoming a gay whale I'd eat at them more often. Well, that and the fact I'd be completely broke. Diners have a little bit of everything, and expect you to be nothing more than awake. That means if you're having a breakdown, a break-up, binge eating, depression eating, or just needing a moment to not be judged, diners are the place for you. And the one of my preference was none other than: Village Inn.

"Oh wow, this place has really changed," I said, taking in the newly renovated decor.

The last time I was in this Village Inn had been so long ago I could only remember vaguely the tacky brown and orange booths and terrible wallpaper. Now it was styled to look like a fifties throw back. The booths and tables all dull blue with orange accents. Gone were the heavy browns, now replaced with light mocha colors. It was a far sight better than the old version of itself but it now lacked the grungy diner appeal I enjoyed.

Putting in our orders a moment of silence fell between the three of us. I knew what question was coming and Rachael had to ask it or be labeled a monster by society.

"How are you doing?" Rachael asked.

There it was, the million dollar question I would likely answer a thousand more times before I was able to be home alone in my apartment.

"Honestly, I'm not ok, but I think I'm fine." It was the truth.

"God, Bri," Rachael also never adopted my name change. "I can't believe she's gone."

"You and me both."

"What happened?"

"I don't have all of the details yet. Right now all I know is she had lung cancer."

"And she didn't tell anyone?"

"I know she told my dad the night before she died, but I haven't talked to the rest of the family. They've been leaving me voicemails, I'm just not ready to deal with them yet."

"How are your brother and sister?"

"I have no idea. The number I have for Jami is out of service and I don't have a number for Jeremy."

"Is there anything I can do to help?" Rachael offered, knowing there's really nothing you can do when someone dies.

"If you can go with me to the funeral home that would be great. That and drink with me when we get back to the hotel."

"I'll call work in the morning and see if they'll let me off. I took most of my sick days for the year already and I have two write-ups. But I'll try."

"Well, even if you can't, at least Dennis is here so if I have to go breakdown in a broom closet he can stall so no one sees me cry."

My joke wasn't going over as well as hoped. Instead of a giggle I was receiving two looks of pity.

Our food arrived by the time I finished the first pot of coffee. Shoveling it in as fast as possible, all I wanted to do was get back to the hotel, kick off my shoes and pound a half dozen beers. Gym be damned, this is one time I'm going back to beer and saying to hell with wine.

Being the great friend that she is, Rachael didn't even question my demand for late night beers. Seeing how my plane landed later than expected and bars stopped serving far too early in Utah, hotel drinking was the only option. Dennis abandoned us for sleep, leaving me and Ray alone in a hotel room.

Filling the kitchen-less room's bathroom sink with ice we packed in the PBR cans. They were already cool but this way we could ensure there was no need to consume piss warm alcohol in an hour. Cracking open the first two, we gave a cheers to Mom and put on Bon Jovi's, 'You Give Love a Bad Name.' Mom loved this song, even though I recall her once arguing with her ex who called it, "Bubble gum rock."

Pulling back the curtains I looked out on the city before me. Everything was so much smaller. From the ninth floor window I could see across much of the city, the biggest building just over thirty floors was a few blocks away. Dim lights glowing, street lights changing every so often. A car would pass every now and then, no honks or horns blaring as would be typical at home. Not a person walking the streets, it's like I'd returned to a vacant city that now only housed me, Rachael and twenty-eight more beers.

5. Reality

Price, Utah is several hours south of Salt Lake City. There's one direct route and it requires driving over a steep set of mountains on a two-lane highway. The drive is constantly made worse as you are bound to get trapped behind a semi-truck hauling god-knows-what across the state in one direction or another.

My dad volunteered to drive me down and as luck would have it, Rachael was able to get the day off from work. Though I'm pretty sure she had to come up with a clever lie to do so. She's called out so often there's no way anyone would believe her if she were to say her gay husband's mother died.

The obsessive planner I am, I contacted my sister to give her a time and place to meet: The funeral home. Technically, I was left in charge of making the arrangements, but as it is with anything involving people, politics need to get involved. Mom had been very clear with her desire to be cremated. Though this wasn't ideal to me, it wasn't my choice and I was committed to ensuring she had what she wanted. You think her last will and testament would be enough; wrong. Because I have siblings, the law requires us all to sign off on the cremation. I was prepared to bulldoze anyone attempting to stop me. Much to my surprise Jami and Jeremy, my siblings, put up no fight. Jami agreeing to meet me there and get in touch with Jeremy.

As the black Jeep pulled into the parking lot, I examined the funeral home. Probably built in the fifties, the place was composed of faded brown bricks. The shingles a few shades darker, looking dry and gritty in the early spring sun. Patches of snow still on the ground in places, not a surprise for Utah, the winter had a way of holding on some years with a lingering bitter cold.

Jeremy and some guy I'd never seen stood outside a maroon minivan taking drags off of rolled cigarettes. Stepping out of the Jeep, my brother approached, coming in for a hug. I gave a one-armed hug in response. I didn't really have a reason to not like my brother. Other than one fist fight when he called me a fag, there'd been no real issues. I think my main problem with him would be his lack of motivation and expectation of handouts from everyone.

Jami came from around the side of the minivan, it was probably her's considering she had two kids and I couldn't conceive of a situation where my brother was the owner of a car.

"Hey, B, how are you?" Jami asked, giving me a hug, her eyes red and puffy.

"Fine considering the circumstances," I replied.

Not in the mood for small talk, I made my way up the six cement steps to the heavy wooden door comprising the building's entrance. Pulling with some force to open the thing and enter a place I would prefer to never know. It looked like a church inside, chairs lined up in chapel formation on the right, lights dimmed. A man appearing from behind a glass door, the closed blinds banging as it shut behind him.

"You must be Brian. I'm Scott, we spoke on the phone yesterday."

"Nice to meet you," I lied, shaking Scott's hand. It really wasn't nice to meet him. In fact, if there was one person I'd prefer to never meet in my life, it would be Scott. Though this is through no fault of his own. He seems like a perfectly nice person.

"If you want to follow me. I have a few papers I need you to sign and then we can finalize things."

With a forced smile, I followed Scott into the room beyond the blind covered glass door. A long conference table was crammed into the space. Scott sat at the head of the table, me to his left, Jeremy on my right, Jami across the table from him. Rachael and my stepmother, Janet, sat on the wall behind me, Dennis and my dad sitting against the wall behind Jami. I recorded these details in my mind as it felt like a moment I would need to reflect upon later.

"I'd like to begin by saying how sorry I am for your loss. There's no easy way to take any of this, but I'll try to make it as easy as possible."

Scott took us through the usual questions, confirming I was the executor of the estate. Looking to my siblings, they both gave their agreement on my taking control. On one hand I wish they'd put up a fight, right now some arguing would probably do me a world of good, but at the same time I enjoy getting my way. I am the youngest sibling after all.

It's possible to think that if you know you are about to die things can be set in order. Assuming this usually happens to people later in life, they may take certain steps to complete paperwork and detail their wishes and remove burden from those they will be leaving behind. Other than a handwritten will and several conversations, Mom really left things up in the air. Going so far as to say I would know what to do.

Then Scott began with the questions. Family first.

"Your mother's father's name?" Scott asked.

My grandfather died when Mom was a kid, I wasn't sure what his name was. Was it Val? I think it may have been.

"Do either of you know?" There was no option but to ask my siblings. Maybe one of them had this nugget of information.

"Val Hannon," Jeremy replied, slumping forward in the chair next to me.

It was important to show strength in this moment, sitting upright and proper, going so far as to wear my glasses to ensure contacts couldn't get my eyes misty by mistake.

"And her mother's name?"

"Lucille. Do you guys know her last name?" This was a bit embarrassing. I don't know the names of the people that birthed my mother.

"Beach, I think," Jami said, wiping at her eyes with the provided box of cheap store brand tissues.

After a dozen more questions we fulfilled enough family history and personal facts to ensure a death certificate could be issued. Then we came to the obituary. Scott asked me to jot a few bullets on a leaf of white paper. I'd never composed an obituary, so I did as he asked and put down a handful notes...covering the front and back of the page. Scott handed the scribbles to a secretary who typed up my bullets in a semi-cohesive manner.

"Oh, if I knew you were using this as is I'd have done a better job," I said, Scott handing me the typed version of my notes. The bullets strung together haphazardly.

"Feel free to make any edits you'd like." Scott would regret these words.

Three rounds later we had a completed obituary, though it would have been faster to just let me type the damn thing on my own. The secretary was slow and quickly getting on my nerves.

"If you want to sign off on the copy here we can submit it to the local papers. If you'd like any of the regional papers included just check the box and they'll contact you with pricing."

"We have to pay for an obituary to be in the paper?" Who knew this wasn't a free service.

"Only if you'd like to have it appear in the Tribune or other regional distribution papers. I should also mention they may not include the word 'bullshit.'"

"If they're going to charge me, they're going to print exactly what I wrote."

Mom was never politically correct. Her obituary was meant to be in the same fashion: Honest and to the point, no time for fluffy lies.

"We're down to the last item and then we can begin viewings. As far as an urn we have a wide selection her for you to pick from."

Scott placed a binder in front of me. Even in death there are many fashionable options for the box you will live in for eternity.

"She asked me to spread her ashes so I don't need anything elaborate."

"If you prefer, we can go with the basic option. This would be the black plastic container that can be easily opened." The 'basic' name was surely a tactic to guilt people into spending more money.

"That's fine. I'd also like a pendant or something on a necklace so I can have a piece of her."

"We have a selection of jewelry here you can pick from."

Glancing over the page, my choice was easy. A sterling silver cylinder. It was simple, pretty and somewhat emotionless.

"Do either of you want one?"

Jami shook her head, Jeremy selecting a chain with some sort of acorn on the end.

"And this one please." Handing the booklet back to Scott our selections had been made.

"Okay, so let me ask, would you like to see your mother?"

"I would. But can you make sure she's covered with a sheet? I don't want to see her that way." I said, nerves rising in the pit of my stomach. What was I about to see?

"Of course. If you decide you would like to view her body, I'd like to ask that you have me pull the sheet back as to not disturb anything."

"What do you mean?" I asked, what could I possibly disturb by pulling the sheet back?

"Because of her condition we want to ensure nothing moves."

"I'm sorry, I'm not understanding. What condition?"

"The exit wound behind her ear. Everything is in place and we want to ensure nothing is moved."

I looked to my dad, his face was red from holding back tears.

"I thought she died of lung cancer. Did she shoot herself?"

No one responded, the entire room silent as the revelation came to life.

"And I'm the only one who didn't know."

Standing, I was enraged, all I wanted to do was put my fist through the wall. How could Dad let me walk into this place not knowing what really happened?

"Fine. I'd like to see my mother now."

6. Why

"Right through here."

Following Scott, we walked into a large viewing room. My heart sank as the lights flickered to life. Twenty-five feet away, under a handmade blanket of green and white checkers was Mom. The last hour and a half I'd not shed a single tear, not flinching for even a moment during the series of uncomfortable questions. It felt at times as though Scott was trying to get tears from me and I wasn't about to cooperate, not with everyone else in the room blubbering like fools.

In this moment though, my walls are shaking and all I want is for Scott to leave and close the damn door. I can feel the emotional falling apart coming on, but I can't let it happen in front of another person, especially not a relative stranger.

"If you need anything please let me know. There are tissues here if you need them." Scott directed me toward a simple silver box on a small wooden table to the left.

Also on the table were tabloid magazines. How wonderfully inappropriate. My mind shifted momentarily to wonder who might actually sit and read a smut magazine while grieving.

"Thank you."

The corrugated wooden door slid shut and I was alone in a room of thin, removable walls. Pulling one of the stiff wooden chairs from the wall I placed it beside Mom and sat.

"Hi, Mom." My voice was shaking, there was no holding back the tears, but it was important to keep my voice down. I could hear the others just beyond the flimsy wall on my left.

"You'll do just about anything to get me to visit," I made a joke with the hope of calming my nerves. "I hate that this happened. I hate that you did this. Why didn't you tell me you were sick?"

Pausing for a moment, my mind tried in frantic desperation to register a response that would never come.

"We could have spent the last few months bar hopping and eating our way around the city. Then you go and do this and leave me here alone."

The tears, impossible to stop, rolling forcefully down both cheeks. My face feeling hot as I did my best to keep the sob sounds from escaping. It felt like choking from the inside out.

"How could you do this? After everything with Aunt Leesa. We agreed to never kill ourselves, you know better than anyone how it fucks everyone up...and you did it anyway."

My Aunt Leesa died seven years earlier. The death was ruled a suicide, but to this day I'm convinced her husband shot her in the head. I mean, how many suicides happen when someone is hiding under the bottom shelf of a linen closet? That doesn't seem ideal for making one's final escape with a shotgun.

After Leesa died, Mom and I were both impacted, she more so than I. But the one thing stemming from that terrible day, I thought, was agreement suicide was not the way out, no matter how bad things became for either of us.

Looking over the bumps in the blanket, Mom was right there but she felt a million miles away. I need her to look at me. I need her to respond to me, and it's not going to happen with her hiding from me under a blanket. Swallowing my tears and releasing a heavy breath I stepped over to the door, sliding it open. Scott was sitting in a chair across the way.

"I need to see her."

Scott stood, walking to me. Before moving to grant him access, I had to know,

"Is everything okay?" I asked, motioning around my head with a hand.

I'd never seen an actual gunshot wound but could imagine the damage it would leave behind.

"Yes, she looks completely normal." An interesting selection of words.

"Okay, I just wanted to be sure."

Scott entered the room, walking up beside the platform where Mom was resting. Gently he folded back the homemade blanket, a white sheet still blocking her from view. With another gentle lift, the sheet was tucked down, revealing her face. I had to take a deep breath, my eyes fixed on the ground while Scott completed his task and once more exited the room, closing the door behind himself.

Summoning courage, or something that felt like courage, I pulled my eyes up, moving forward reluctantly. She looked peaceful in a way I'd never seen her in life. She was thinner than the last time we'd been together, but I guess that's to be expected.

"You promised me thirty years, and you only gave me two."

On more than one occasion Mom mentioned not wanting to get old and fall apart. I told her I needed thirty more years of her time and then I'd be mature enough to let her go.

"You promised." The tears back in full force. "You were supposed to move to New York so we could get old and sit in bars drinking together. Now who's going to make fun of people with me? Who am I going to call when people piss me off, or when I need to tell you something really funny that's just happened?"

This moment, this was the end, this was the goodbye. The minutes feeling incredibly short, ticking by as I tried to cram every thought I could possibly conceive into this moment. If I don't say it now, there's no other opportunity. It really is now or never. We didn't have any big secrets and Mom knew everything about me there was to know, most of which was pretty mundane, but this was my only chance to talk to her. The only chance to see her face before it would be gone forever.

"I'm so mad at you for leaving like this."

If I'd ignored all of the phone calls from yesterday this could all be a lie which never happened. Maybe it's only real because I'm standing in the middle of it with open eyes.

"I love you and I'm going to miss you forever. There will never be anyone like you, and no one will ever understand me the way you did. I feel empty without you. But I hope you're in a better place."

I wonder if she can hear me. If there is a God and a heaven, can loved ones hear the pleas we leave with them as they depart? Or, if there is a heaven, is it so blissful to escape our reality that the person never looks back for a single second? I hope the second one. It would be better to be so blissfully happy that you can never regret leaving. Unfortunately this doesn't help me, or the way I feel in this moment.

"I have to go. I won't get to see you again, but I love you and I'm so sorry things turned out this way. I guess we really don't get to control everything in life."

Afraid to get too close, I rested my hand briefly on the blanket where I could see the outline of her hand. I have to let go.

"I'm done." Sliding the door shut behind myself and wiping off my face, Scott stood.

"Would you like me to let any of the others say goodbye?" Scott asked.

"Yes, if they'd like to."

While others took turns to pay their respects and make peace, I paced the chapel. All I wanted to do was run screaming from this place. Holding myself together with such force made it feel as though I was going to burst from my skin in a fit of insanity. I was in desperate need of a drink and a dark bar to cry.

7. Collateral

Every choice we make has consequences. As most of us consider our personal feelings when it comes to a decision, we don't think with regularity on how a choice may impact those around us. For example, when I was four or so years old, my parents divorced. This was a result of an affair my mother had.

Both of my parents would remarry. My dad, Red, met his second wife through a woman with which he and Mom were both friends. Patsy was her name and she worked for a cliché, big-breasted, blonde lady who ran a nail salon. Setting the blonde and Red, Dad, up on a blind date, Patsy soon reconsidered the decision based on Mechelle's, that's the blonde, tumultuous relationship history. Her efforts to halt the relationship didn't go far as she was immediately unemployed and exiled form the friendship.

The reality: Red was smitten with Mechelle and there was nothing that could be done to stop their courtship. Not even the shared knowledge that his soon-to-be bride had already walked down the aisle six, or was it seven, times before their meeting. He was quickly in love and introducing me to the woman that would become my stepmother...for a long seven years.

Had my mother never had an affair perhaps the two would have remained married. Though this would have been highly unlikely. Opposites attract, but when your personalities are dramatically opposite the relationship is doomed to fail. In the same sense however, my stepmother inspired me to work harder. She once told me how she thought I would never be able to graduate from college. From that moment I worked even harder in school to ensure I could shove success down her throat. Unfortunately, she wasn't around by the time I graduated high school or college. Though I hear she's on husband nine these days. Good for her. How unfortunate for him.

Even when we make a final decision, like the pulling of a trigger, there is going to be collateral damage. Sally, a woman I'd heard of in conversation several times, but never met had retrieved my phone number from a note left behind by Mom. She reached out to let me know she had Mom's apartment and car keys, as well as a few possessions she'd been asked to put in her safe.

Escaping the funeral home, Red drove us all to Sally's home. She'd mentioned Mom's apartment was just around the corner from her. Though I'd need directions as Google doesn't even know where the hell we are and I've never been to this middle-of-nowhere place.

Rent (minus) Control: Bulletproof

The moment my foot hit the ground I heard a screen door open. One thing about small towns, people are always looking out the window. So when a truck full of strange people pulls up to your house you'll either be welcomed or run off with a loaded weapon.

"You must be Brian."

"On a good day."

"It's nice to meet you dear. I'm Sally."

Sally looked to be in her fifties maybe even a touch older. Her long hair was brushed, but the brown, lined with gray was unruly and clearly didn't enjoy being straight. Had she been in New York with the humidity I'm sure it would poof into a white person afro. She dressed in a casual manner that resembled Mom, jeans and a long sleeve t-shirt, nothing fancy. Her face was tan from working in her garden, though the warm days of spring are still some time away.

"Come on in, I have some papers for you."

Wonderful, more papers.

"Do you mind if I use your restroom quickly?" I asked. "It was a long ride and I didn't even think to go when we last stopped."

"Sure, dear. First door on your left over there."

Sally's house was an update on the log cabin, rustic on the outside but filled with the amenities of life on the inside. She was clearly a collector of...well, everything. Shelves hung in the bathroom with a dozen different pigs on them. Costume jewelry of every color draped over a series of hooks beside the mirror above the sink. In the window sat several frogs, two of which looked to be having tea with one another.

As I washed and dried my hands, pulling open the door, I noticed more knickknacks on shelves all over the living and dining rooms. Sally clearly watched a lot of QVC as I'm pretty sure half of their collections from the last decade were stacked on end tables and narrow bookcases.

"These are the keys to your mom's apartment. I don't want you to worry, I went over to make sure the bedroom was cleaned up before you got here."

The bedroom, that's where it happened. It makes sense. A bed is one of the most comfortable and safe pieces of furniture you can own. Even as a child I would hide under the covers, pulling them tightly around my head to ensure I was safe from whatever was lurking in the closet. Too bad my bed is thousands of miles away, now seems like a great time to plunge under the covers and hide.

"I also have her car keys. Right now the car is in my garage. I didn't want Cort to show up and try hauling it off. Your mom didn't want him to have that car."

Rent (minus) Control: Bulletproof

A little over a year ago, Mom and her boyfriend of seven years, Cort, split ways. Cort started having an affair with his so called high school sweetheart or as he referred to her, *'the love of his life.'* This ended their relationship and is the reason Mom lived in an apartment in this strange town. My infrequent visits meant I'd never been to see the place. Though now I wish I'd made more of an effort and not protested so much last Christmas when she asked me to come.

The only lingering piece of the relationship Mom and Cort have is her car. Purchased new, the car was originally in both their names, but after the relationship dissolved Mom kept the car and made the payments. As I'd been told, Cort was to sign over the title to her in full once the car loan was paid. Which in terms of monthly payments would be within the next year.

"But most important, I need to give you this." Sally said, her eyes a bit misty as she held out a large manila envelope.

"What is it?" I asked, not immediately reaching for the thing.

"A few important numbers...and a note...to you."

Accepting the envelope I pulled up the flap to peer inside. Was something going to jump out and bite me? It felt as much.

"I hope you don't mind, I read it," confessed Sally.

"It's fine," I said, tucking the envelope under my arm. "Would you mind showing us where the apartment is? We need to start clearing things out while I have everyone available."

"Of course. If you want to follow me in your truck I'll show you now."

Piling back into Red's truck we followed Sally. While I had a moment to myself I pulled a piece of photocopied paper from the envelope. Apparently when the original was collected by the police they felt I was only deserving of a photocopy. There on the paper, the final goodbye I was waiting to receive.

Brian I love you!
Jeremy I Love you!

Do well my babies. You are the best thing I ever did. Never forget that. I'm tired and I want to be with the rest of them.

It will be okay, it's just time, you will always be in my heart. Look for me, I'm always going to be with you. I will always watch over you.

Love, Mom

My boys get what I have. Brian is my best to decide.

P.S. Cort can't have the car.

Brian cremate me and spread the remains.

Looking away from the others to hide the tears on my face I noticed an additional note tucked under some other papers.

Sally, Call Red.

Please look after Goldie. Thank you for being my friend.

Sally - tell Cort to fuck off!

8. Possessions

Before rushing over to Sally's, Red, made a very important stop: The State Liquor Store. In Utah, you can only buy wine and other delicious treats from a state controlled chain of stores. No matter, I secured a magnum bottle of red wine, knowing I would likely need it for motivation over the next few hours.

And for those who wonder why people call my dad, Red, it's pretty obvious. He has true ginger hair, but with a twist, it's almost the length of his entire back. When I was a teenager most of my friends thought he looked rough, tough and scary. Once they met him and realized what a nice guy he is their opinions quickly changed. Making our house a popular hangout, which in high school is one of the most important things.

Handing the apartment keys to Red, I climbed down from the passenger's seat. The height of the truck meant climbing onto the edge of the tire to reach into the back and retrieve the jug of wine I was committed to consuming; with or without help.

The fading white brick apartment complex was made up of four units. Two at ground level, the other two stacked above. The group of helpers stood perched at the top of the stairs, climbing the concrete stairs, I was stopped three steps from the top.

"What are we waiting on?" I asked, wine properly wrapped in my arms like a precious child.

"We need the keys," Sally explained, standing in front of the door.

"Where's my dad? I gave them to him."

I hauled back down the stairs to find Red shuffling around inside the now open trailer hitched to his truck.

"Can I have the keys back?"

"I gave them to your sister."

Instantly becoming frustrated, I pulled my head from the trailer. Jami was still getting her things together inside the truck cabin.

"Do you have the apartment keys?" I asked, trying to hold on to my calm.

"I gave them to Sally. Or wait, maybe I put them in my bag."

This is like a fucking stress test. How can a set of keys become lost in less than five minutes? That's what I get for letting them out of my sight and trusting others to be responsible.

"I found them," called Sally, from the top of the stairs.

Swallowing the frustration and anger I once more climbed the aging concrete steps and entered the apartment. This was my first time in this place but everything was familiar. The furniture, the photos on the wall, the placement of coasters on the coffee table and a crocheted blanket on the arm of the couch. Everything in this place was her.

Pushing past everyone and into the kitchen which opened from the side of the living room, I placed the wine on the table, searching for the plastic cups I knew would be somewhere in the blue cabinets. As I looked I noticed an IKEA chalkboard hanging on the wall to the left of the stove.

Where you'd expect to see a grocery list or recipes scrawled in white chalk there was a drawing. A multicolored drawing I'd done years ago as a spoof of where I once lived in Brooklyn. The slanted building, a faux L Train sign, my stick figure head poking up from the steps of the basement apartment, and of course, a crack dealer on the corner. Not once had I thought of this after the Christmas visit when I'd drawn the thing. But here it was preserved for all these years. Not even a single smudge mark in all the chalk.

"You okay, B?" Jami asked, touching the back of my shoulder.

Grumbling a 'yes' I returned from the land of make-believe and chalk. Locating a stack of plastic red picnic cups, I sat five on the table in a line. It didn't really matter if anyone had a drink with me. In fact, I could care less if they did or didn't. But before I take apart this apartment, it's important to toast the person to whom it belongs. Filling the cups, mine a little more so than was probably reasonable; Jami, Janet and Sally all took up a cup.

"To Mom," I said, taking a massive swig of the cheap and pungent wine.

"Cheers," their voices rang in unison.

Refilling my cup it was time to do a quick lap around the apartment. Everyone was standing in the living room waiting for direction. Doing a rough inventory, we had our work cut out for us. The two bedroom apartment was twice the size of mine in New York. On one occasion Mom mentioned her spare bedroom as being 'full of shit' and she wasn't joking. The spare room was stacked with items that had no place or were retrieved from the house she once shared with the ex-boyfriend. It was almost enough to get us on an episode of Hoarders.

Speaking to no one in particular and to everyone at once,

"Here's what I would like to have happen. Dad, Jeremy, Dennis if you guys can get the bigger items like the sofa and this big recliner out, they can all go into the trailer and be donated.

The tables and entertainment center can all go as well. Then we'll have some space to start sorting and boxing things here in the living room."

Turning I was about to walk away when a thought occurred.

"If anyone would like to keep something, just ask. I'm happy to give everything a good home especially the things that will be donated."

With that we began the task of disassembling the apartment. Seeing as gossip travels at immense speed through small towns, a knock came from the open door as the first few items were being hauled out and loaded into the truck. A dark haired woman who looked strangely familiar and a sandy-haired teenager were at the door.

"Can I help you?" I asked, thumbing through a drawer full of papers, hoping to not overlook anything of importance.

"Brian, I'm your mom's cousin, Stephanie. This is my son, Jesse."

"Right," I muttered, pretending this triggered a memory.

Stephanie looked familiar but that could be the amount of my mother present in her face. The last time we'd been in the same room I was probably a toddler. So name and face recognition aren't doing much for me at this moment in time.

"I wanted to stop by and talk to you for a minute...if that's alright."

Annoyed by the interruption, I followed Stephanie into the kitchen. The Hannon family trademark dark hair with large, loose curls, that's why she looked so much like Mom. I could even see a bit of resemblance in the eyes. The one trait that seems to hold from one person to the next in this family with certainty is the blue eyes and tired look they carry.

"This probably isn't a great time to ask, but I wanted to know if Jesse could have the washer and dryer? Your mom just loved him and always watched out for him. We're going to miss her so much."

Expecting pleas for sympathy, it didn't come off as frustrating or even much of a surprise the first family members to make an appearance were only after items.

"If you can get them out of the bathroom, they're yours," I said, taking a shot of wine from whoever's cup had been abandoned on the kitchen table.

Getting back to my sorting of the side table shoved full of old pay stubs and random notes on torn papers, Jesse came up beside me.

"I'm really sorry to hear about your mom."

"Thanks," I said, not looking up, my glasses sliding down my nose. I wasn't sure if they or he was more irritating.

"Can I do anything to help?" Jesse asked, looking truly depressed as I noted his face for the first time since he traipsed over.

Reining in my abrasive attitude, I stood up straight, glancing around the room.

"You know what would be great," I said, trying to use my light retail voice. "If you could go through the cabinets of the entertainment center. The movies can all be donated unless you'd like any of them. The CD's if you can put them in a box for me, I'll need those later."

"Sure, no problem."

And just like that, Jesse was another pair of hands.

Over the next four hours I was asked a hundred different times and ways if, *'I can take this,'* and *'It would mean so much to have this.'* There wasn't a single item I denied to anyone. I knew it would do me no good to hold on to everything and it was also impossible. I was also keenly aware Mom would rather someone who needs something, or is going to get use from an item, take it home. So that is how I judged each piece.

Before long the entire apartment was empty. The last boxes went down the stairs and the poor cat, Miss Goldie Hawn, who I had locked in the bathroom for safekeeping, was crated and placed in the truck. I didn't know exactly what to do with the cat, but for now she was coming with us back to Salt Lake. Taking a final lap around the apartment to ensure everything was collected and not a single memory overlooked, I noticed something.

When we first entered the apartment I'd been in such a rush I'd barely noticed the bed. The mattress had been hauled away by a professional cleaning crew before my arrival, but now the bed frame itself was gone and the room empty, there was something I'd not noticed before. On the wall behind the place where a head would have rested was a faint, erratic pattern of red. The cleaners had clearly not been as thorough as one would hope.

I ran my fingers over the dried blood. It was surreal. This was as close to being a part of that terrible last moment as I was going to come. It wasn't upsetting as you might think, in a way it made the situation real.

My moment of silent reflection was short lived.

"B, we're ready to go," Jeremy said, poking his head into the room.

"Alright."

Making a final exit, I closed both of the bedroom doors and the bathroom door. It was like a final check on my mental to-do list.

"I just want to say something before we all leave," Jeremy said, his hands tucked into jean pockets concealed by an oversized hoodie. "We haven't been close, but we should all make an effort to stick together now that Mom's gone."

"I just want to say, I love you guys," Jami added.

The pair looked at me. Apparently, I was expected to say something to reassure and comfort them, but I can't lie and I have no words of comfort left in me.

"Sure, love you guys too," I said, allowing a quick hug before we left the apartment and I pulled shut the door, locking it one final time.

9. Postcards

Here's an idea: Why can't we make the process of taking care of a loved one's final documents and processing their remains a one-stop thing? Think of it this way. Instead of going to a funeral home to fill out paperwork, coming back for a viewing, assuming there's a funeral, then going to a cemetery and coming back again to finish things, make it quick and easy. Let the family fill out paperwork, and if there is to be no funeral, process the remains and let us get on with our lives.

No, this is not how things work. As it takes two days to complete a cremation, meaning Dennis and I are trapped in the world of my former and mostly repressed life.

Arriving at a hotel in downtown Salt Lake City, a long three hour drive from Price, Red and Janet decided to stay with us for a bit before heading home. It would take them another hour to get home from here. It was too late to go to the bar, but as luck would have it the hotel two buildings over has a cafe that is open and still serving alcohol. Perhaps there is a god and in this one moment he is taking pity on grieving souls. That, or it just so happens the hotel is run by a hardcore drunk. Really, either is fine with me.

"Can I get a Sam Adams, please?" I asked the Latino gentleman behind the register.

"Sure, can I see your ID?"

Reaching for my back pocket it became immediately clear there was no wallet to be found.

"Crap, I left it in the room," I said, knowing how this was going to play out. "Do I need it?"

"We ID everyone?"

"Really, because you didn't ask him when he ordered a beer?" I said, pointing out the elderly man who had just taken a seat at a table behind us, ordering a drink moments before.

"Sorry, I need an ID."

"Can you bend the rules?" I pleaded. "What if I told you that my mother died this week and I just spent the evening clearing out every possession she had from her apartment and hauling them off in a truck."

"Sorry, I need an ID."

"Just my luck. We're in the one state that actually enforces the stupid ID rule."

Annoyed I walked away from the counter and found a table with enough chairs for all of us to sit comfortably.

Fortunately, Rachael, who was planning to have a slumber party with me, ordered a beer we could share since the stingy counter guy wouldn't oblige my request.

The others gathered around the table. We were all emotionally and physically drained from what may be the longest day of my life. Everything on my checklist for the day was done. Now we had to wait for the ashes to be ready and, last but not least, plan a wake. That would be tomorrow's challenge.

"I just want to say your mom was a tough person and I'm glad I had the chance to know her." Red held up his glass, we raised ours in her honor. "And I wanted to give you this. Thought they might make you feel better."

Taking a sip, Red placed his glass on the table and pulled from Janet's massive purse a large zip bag full of papers.

"What is it?" I asked, accepting the plastic container.

Immediately I knew what was in my hands.

"They're the postcards your mom used to send you."

During my early teen years, Mom drove a truck over-the-road, or long haul, with her husband of the time. This meant there were sometimes two, three even four weeks where we didn't see each other. Cell phones weren't what they are today and we would have short calls with the phone cards she mailed me. My stepmother at the time, not Janet, didn't allow me to make long-distance calls. My god, she was such a hateful cunt. The best decision Red ever made was getting rid of that woman.

There was a stack of postcards in my closet at home, I'd not thought of them until now, and I didn't realize so many had been left behind. Pulling them from the bag, they were every shape and size. There must have been thirty or forty of the colorful pieces of stocky paper. Each one from a different city. A vibrant beach in Florida, a pig farm in Kansas, some sort of field in Illinois.

Turning them over, each had a message scrawled on the back. The handwriting unnervingly familiar. The curves in the letters, the large cursive *'Love Mom'* at the bottom of each. My own handwriting was similar, large curves, ignoring the lines and always making a loud statement with the signature.

Reading card after card it was in this moment that all of the walls I was hiding behind for the last two days came crumbling to the ground with an intense thrust. Unwilling to let the others see me cry, I folded my head down toward the table. Doing my best to swallow the sobs.

"It's gonna be okay," Janet said, moving behind me to offer what comfort she could.

Appreciative of the gesture, I didn't swat her away as would be my normal reaction to someone trying to comfort me.

"I ju-just d-d-don't under-stand h-how I'm su-su-pp-posed to g-get over th-this." My thoughts were clear but the words just couldn't hold together through the tears.

Throwing caution to the wind I looked up, taking an enormous gulp from the beer bottle, the counter guy giving me bitter brown eyes. There wasn't a dry eye at the table. My tears were infectious and no one had the strength to ward them off.

"Wh-what am I go-going t-to do wi-with-out h-her?"

"It's going to be hard," Janet said, leaning down to hug me now that I was in an upright position in the chair. "My brother passed not long ago and I still think about him every day."

"Th-this wasn't what was supposed to h-happen," I declared, beginning to regain composure. "I thought we h-had so m-much m-more time."

"I know, sweetie."

"Did you know it wasn't just the cancer?" I asked looking to Red, his face flushed, eyes teary.

"The police told me when they called. I was hoping you wouldn't have to hear it and have that picture in your head," he admitted.

"How long did you know she had cancer?"

"She told me the night she died. She called, drunk, and told me. But she made me promise not to tell you she had cancer. She didn't want you to worry."

"So was this a planned suicide or do you think it just happened?" Why would she make him promise not to tell me about the cancer if she was going to kill yourself a few hours later? It didn't make any sense.

"I don't know, son. Maybe she had one too many and it seemed like a good idea."

"I told her it wasn't a good idea for people like us to own guns. See what happens. We are *too* crazy to have guns."

Another hour of drinking and shedding tears over postcards and the lady from the front desk, in her crisply pressed cranberry colored shirt was ushering us into the street. It was well beyond midnight and I was far from drunk. It was time to give up on this day and call it a night. Fortunately, tomorrow would be an all new day to attempt a sufficient buzz that may have the power to drown out the voices in my head.

10. Scouting

The sun rose over Salt Lake, creeping across the windowsill and between the unclosed curtains. Waking as the heat on my face became intensely irritating, I slung my feet off the bed, rising with some difficulty, making my way to the bathroom. Rachael and I had polished off another dozen cans of beer before watching cartoons and falling asleep in a fit of laughter the night prior. This is what friends are for in life.

The downside of the cheap, low-alcohol content, Utah beer is the amount it causes you to urinate. Made worse as my bladder size appears to be that of a below average size thimble. A flush and relief. Unable to use the sink to wash my hands, several cans of beer floating in what was once ice to remind of the evening's events, I made the decision to draw a bath.

Climbing into the steaming tub I collected the thoughts dancing around my mind. If any moment in life has ever felt surreal, this is the one. Able to feel the bags under my puff riddled eyes, body aching from a hard, uncomfortable hotel bed and flat pillows designed to strain the neck. Suddenly, it was clear I was an adult. The physical pains demonstrating the unpleasant truth of anyone trying to behave like a juvenile in an effort to avoid reality.

Having always felt like a perpetual seventeen-year-old, birthdays never struck any real fear or frustration. At one time I eagerly awaited turning twenty-five. Once you're twenty-five there is nothing in the world you can't do, as this age is when you can rent a car. In American culture this is the final rite of passage. Not that this truly matters, considering I never drive, it's the freedom of no restriction. Now, with three decades of existence behind me and life altering events coming to fruition it is clear I'm on my own. Seventeen could not feel more far away from this moment.

Not to say I'm actually alone. There are plenty of friends who will let me cry on their shoulders, or more realistically, cry in a beer across the table from them. But it always seemed as though there was an invisible safety net to catch me if anything were to ever happen. Mom was the net. With her gone it means falling will be met with the cold and uncompromising ground. Not to say Red won't help me in a pinch, but it's just not the same. I'm a momma's boy.

The water began lapping at my chest as the tub filled, water falling heavy from the silver faucet decorated by hard water stains. Curls of steam rising into the air and beginning to fog over the large mirror hanging above the sink. Staring at the tattoo on my right peck, I traced the lines of the Brooklyn Bridge with my fingertips.

The vision for this tattoo was always clear. I wanted one tower of the bridge, looking from Brooklyn to Manhattan. Every visit to New York she made, Mom insisted we walk from Brooklyn to Manhattan, which we did. The bridge was the first city landmark we saw together, walking across during a cold, misty morning rain. When I told her about my idea for a new tattoo, Mom had a suggestion of her own. Add 'MOM' somewhere into the base of the tower. Declining, it seemed tacky to add the letters. Now I wished they were there. Even if only to stand as a reminder of this one simple story.

Rising from the tub, water rushed off my flesh, splashing around and pooling on the floor. Twisting the handle to stop the flow of water and uncorking the drain, I reached for a towel. That's when we made eye contact. Me and the person standing in the mirror holding the same towel. Who the hell is that? The stress, frustration and sadness spread across a face that was now worn and exhausted. There was no way to hide what was happening.

"Panda husband," Rachael called, knocking on the door. "Let me in, I have to pee."

Pulling on a pair of black boxer briefs, I unlocked the door, pulling it open so Rachael could enter. Coming in, she dropped the pajama pants decorated in pink skulls and cross bones.

"Oh, *thank god*, I was about to explode," she said, sucking at the end of an electronic cigarette.

There was something about Rachael you had to love. She didn't care what anyone thought. Her style was somewhere between goth and hipster, though I'd never say this to her. Call Rachael a hipster and she may light you on fire. Her tattoos, covering nearly every inch of available flesh, beautifully composed. A strong exterior for a person with a compassionate heart and a bleeding soul for animals.

"Do you have to work today?"

"I have to go in this afternoon or I'll get a point."

"I hate your job."

"Me too. Let's run off and become hookers."

"If my knees were in better shape, I'd be right there with you."

"What are you going to do today?" Rachael asked, pulling up her pants.

"I need to find a big bar with a juke box."

"Can't you drink here in the room and listen to music on your phone?"

"It's not for me," I chuckled, though the argument was persuasive. "My mom said more than once she didn't want a funeral. She wanted a party with rock music. So we need a big bar with a juke box. I was going to play her CDs but then I have to keep track of them and it's too much hassle."

"There's a pub on State Street. Hold on, I can look it up."

Rachael flopped on the bed, flipping black hair out of her face, retrieving a charging phone from the nightstand.

"Poplar Street Pub, that's it. If you do something in the day it will be empty and the place is huge. I don't know if they have a juke box, but there are some games in the back."

"That works and saves me the time of running around. I don't know any good bars here."

"Who are you planning to invite?"

"I figure I'll invite the family members who keep calling me. I don't know any of her friend's phone numbers because the police still have the cell phone. Maybe I can post it to her Facebook page. Would that be weird?"

"No, it's not weird. They'll probably see it that way."

Rachael left for work, leaving me alone in the room. Rather than pester Dennis it seemed worthwhile to walk over to Poplar Street Pub and see if the place would suffice for the occasion. It was only about half a mile and the time to myself was needed.

What a difference a walk in Salt Lake is from New York. Sidewalks nearly empty, no car horns blaring, though crossing the extra wide streets was potentially deadly as no one is watching for pedestrians. It's probably assumed I'm a drug addict or homeless by the passing cars filled with people, even though I'm not dressed in rags. Those are just the stereotypes of people who would usually be walking the streets in this city.

Reaching the pub, it was barely opening, apparently even the hardcore drunks in Utah waited until late afternoon to get their buzz on. That or the law stating no alcohol can be served before noon. Fools.

"Hey, Hun, can I get you a beer?" Asked a blonde, bump-it wearing, bartender who was cleaning a table.

"Can I get a Bud Light...please?"

Waiting for the beer I glanced around. The front portion of the pub was huge, eight heavy wooden tables on the left, chairs all around. A massive pool table on the right with a small stage for local musical acts to strut their stuff. Heading toward the bar, tucked behind an unusual half wall as if this portion of the building had recently been added, I continued to explore the space.

"Thank you," I said, retrieving the beer waiting at the edge of the bar, leaving a wrinkled ten dollar bill.

Two small bathrooms in the corner and a door leading to a massive patio area. The bartender passed me, making her way to the patio, she began raising the umbrellas over the many circular plastic tables.

Another doorway and down two steps I found the games Rachael mentioned. Another massive room, a few two-person tables along one wall. Two more pool tables in the center, arcade games in the back...and there to my amazement and joy was an electronic juke box. Not only was it what I wanted, it would have every song I could ever wish to play. This place was too perfect.

Rent (minus) Control

All that was left now was to send out an invitation and hope the people I need to see it will. This wake is going to go one of two ways: Either it will be overflowing with people or, *worse*, it's going to be me and a handful of relatives crying in a corner as strangers look on in confusion.

11. Dust

When the mortuary called to tell me Mom's ashes were ready to be picked up I sat silently with the phone pressed against my ear. Whomever was on the other phone repeatedly said, 'hello' as I didn't respond. It was so casual for them, they did this sort of thing all the time. Like a pizza delivery person calling to let you know your order is on the way. Did he want me to thank him?

I asked Rachael to drive me back to Price where the mortuary was located to collect the ashes, she had to work. Why isn't one of us independently wealthy and able to support us both? It's not that I didn't want Red to take me, it's just he's already had to deal with enough of the burden. Having to break the news of this particular death to me clearly took a toll on him and I couldn't imagine how it felt. With no other option, I asked for the ride, and as expected, there was no objection.

The drive: Winding, narrow roads, going up and down, hill after hill. Patches of snow, dead fields, the random animal grazing partially edible grass. This desolate place was everything I was feeling in this moment. As cliché as it may be, the distance from my city and any city is immense. Nothing for miles. Everything around more or less dead, and if not dead, not far from death. This is where things come to an end.

Finally arriving at the mortuary it was as bleak as I remembered. Pulling the heavy door open for what would hopefully be the last time, I entered. Scott, the friendly neighborhood mortician, immediately appeared from a corner, there must be a camera or bell you can't hear upon entry as it's astonishing how an employee always pops up.

"How are you today?" Scott asked, extending a hand to shake.

"I'm fine, thanks." If you want me to lie to your face, I'll oblige.

"I have everything ready for you."

Scott led us across the elongated room of 1980's wood paneling and terrible yellow carpeting. If I had to have my funeral here I'd be glad I was dead on arrival. A slender table stood against a window, sunlight burrowing in as if Snow White and chirping birds were about to burst out of the adjacent darkness mid chorus.

Picking up the box it was heavier than I expected. A simple sticker on top: *Patricia Hannon Gartrell. April 24, 1961 - March 2, 2014.*

"You mentioned you will be spreading the ashes," Scott began. "The lid pops open, but it does take a little force."

Running a finger over the lip of the black container's top, it folded in on itself, creating a sort of self-locking clip.

"The cremains are in a plastic bag that can be easily opened."

Cremains...it sounds like there's a berry flavored treat inside the unwanted black box.

"Be sure to keep the bag low to the ground. The cremains can easily catch the wind and make it more difficult to spread them smoothly."

"That's good to know." This was becoming a fun facts of death session.

"Now, I do want to warn you, there may be some familiar items in the cremains."

"What?" A vision of a ringed finger rolling out popped into my mind.

"Sometimes small fragments of bone are still visible."

"Oh, ok. I thought you meant actual pieces...pieces I may know." Teeth are bones. Is it possible teeth could be in the bag?

"No, no, nothing like that."

"The good news is I definitely won't recognize any of her bones." A stone face greeted my remark.

"One last thing," Scott held out a large manila envelope. "Inside you'll find the death certificate with the extra copies you requested, as well as a copy of the obituary."

"Great, thanks so much."

Leaving Scott and the mortuary, Red, Dennis and I piled back into the black Jeep. The car looked like it was made for off-road driving. Enormous tires, polished rims, roll bars all around. If the day's vicious wind pushed us off the road we'd all surely survive.

"Where to?" Red asked.

"She asked to be spread on her father's grave. It's in Monroe Cemetery...I'm not exactly sure where that is." Grabbing my phone, I began to search, the small town presenting me with only a single bar of service.

"Don't worry, I know where it is," Red added, backing out of the parking lot and redirecting us onto the expressway.

Western States are large, mostly empty, expanses of space. Rolling hills, distant snowcapped peaks, and miles of unending pavement. The drive to the cemetery where a dozen family members I'd never met had been laid to rest took nearly two hours.

Upon arrival we were welcomed by a simple cemetery in the middle of nowhere. Driving along the dirt road into the miniature cemetery, surrounded by a rusted chain-link fence to distinguish the space from the neighboring trailer homes.

Checking an aging map just through the entrance, Red located where the tombstone we needed should live. Walking, plastic urn in hand, the bitter air pulled at my face.

"Here it is," Red yelled, Dennis and I walking to him.

On the ground, a flat, aging stone read: *Val Hannon*. This was the guy.

"Wow, he died in sixty-four?" It felt right to ask the question, though the answer was already etched in stone.

I'd discovered an old key when cleaning out Mom's apartment. There was no way of knowing if it went to anything, but it was interesting enough for me to put in my pocket. Now, using the key I'd found by chance, I popped open the top of the urn. The black plastic of the container resisted, asking me to reconsider and leave the resting ashes inside.

Another thrust and the top popped open. A tied bag, full of a chalky gray ash, like something you'd find in the bottom of an old fireplace. I could hear Dad behind me, emotion getting the best of him. If I was to look at him directly it was almost certain I would begin to cry.

Kneeling beside the tombstone of a grandfather whom I'd never known, I opened the bag of ashes and gently poured them around the edges. Leaving a small amount in the bag I tied it off and returned the cremains to the urn, locking the top back in place.

"Bye, Mom." There was really nothing else to say.

Another forty minute drive and we were in the town of Richfield where my parents first met. Having quietly sat for so much time I needed to speak, if only to distract myself from the thought that the ashes were now gone forever.

"How did her dad, I mean, how did Val die?" I asked, wondering if Red retained any information.

"His girlfriend shot him?"

This got my attention.

"What do you mean?" I probed.

"He left his wife, your grandma, for this Mexican woman. But when the girlfriend found out he was also cheating on her, she came home with a shotgun and that was the end."

"Holy shit."

"Yeah, there's no lack of crazy in that family."

"Thank god I'm only half that crazy."

"We're all crazy," Red smiled, the car slowly rolling through Main Street.

"What about you two, how did you and my mom ever meet? It's not like you grew up in the same place"

"I was down here working at the time. Back then there were oil rigs here. I was actually living in that hotel right there."

The Jeep passed by a rundown motel, probably exactly the same today as it was thirty odd years ago when Red was living there.

"So, how did you two end up meeting?"

"Your mom's friend introduced us at the bar. She didn't give me the time of day. Then a few weeks later I asked her out. We ended up dating and eventually she moved into the motel with me."

"How did that work?"

"Work had me down here for six weeks at a time and then I'd head back to Salt Lake for a few days."

"When did you guys move to Salt Lake?"

"We actually lived here until you were born. We couldn't afford a crib so we would put a blanket in the drawer for you."

"Wait, you raised me Chinese style in a drawer?"

"It's all we had," Red laughed at my shock.

"Crap, I knew we were poor, but I didn't know we were drawer baby poor."

"It didn't last long. Once the rigs started closing down we moved to Salt Lake and that's when I got a job with the state."

This was the first time I'd ever asked about my parent's story of coming together. There wasn't a reason why I'd never asked prior, but I now thought to myself how odd it was that I had never been curious when all I ever did was ask questions. If it was possible to go back in time, I would love the opportunity to meet my twenty-something parents. Between the three of us I'm sure we would have been able to have an amazing, drunken time.

12. Awakening

Having never hosted a wake, it wasn't an event I had a full knowledge of how to execute. The only things I know to be required are beer and rock music. With those provided by the bar it was up to Facebook to draw the crowd. Logging into Mom's account, I shared a brief update:

My mother made it clear she wanted her life to be celebrated, specifically with 80's rock music and delicious beverages. To honor her request we will hold a wake at Poplar Street Pub in Salt Lake City, Utah. You will need to be 21 years of age to enter and have a valid ID with you. Food and drink are available for purchase on site. We invite you to come have a drink in honor of Pat Gartrell and celebrate her life.

Hoping my post was enough to lure in those close to Mom I came up with a way for people to memorialize her. From the local Target I purchased a massive photo album, putting together a dozen pages of photos that would surely cause a few tears, but with the real intent of reminding others of all the happy times. The album was harder to create than anticipated. Mom spent all her time behind the camera, there are very few photos of her.

I also grabbed some colored pens and large sheets of clean white paper. Laying the paper out on the table in front of the photo album, I posted a note for anyone to share a memory if they would like to do so.

With everything in place and the guests hopefully beginning to arrive in the next few minutes, I shoved a twenty into the juke box and selected dozens of songs. Everything in Utah, including music, is cheaper than New York. My queue must be at least two hours long. Selecting the final AC/DC song my money would allow, Aunt Sherrie and Uncle Scott appeared from around the corner.

Mom's only surviving siblings, they'd been feuding for years over Scott's wife and Sherrie's dislike of her. At least that's how I'd heard it through the grapevine.

Mustering my retail face and a perky voice, I greeted them each with a hug and a hello.

"How are you doing?" Sherrie asked. She looked like mom through the eyes, though her hair was much lighter.

"As good as I can hope to be," I answered honestly. "I'm glad you both made it, I know it's a long drive."

"We weren't going to miss this," Scott added. "Have you met my wife?" A stout woman appeared from behind Scott.

"Yeah, we met a year or so back when I was in town."

"We did?" She questioned, her jolly face masking any sadness.

We had met, but I'd forgotten her name and no one was offering it up. Why didn't I just lie and say we'd never met? Was it Janice...JoAnne...? The meeting was easy to remember. Mom and I sat on the front porch of their home drinking beers somewhere in the middle of nowhere. I watched the clock as they chatted until finally we left. Pretty standard behavior for people living in that part of the country.

"Are you Brian?" Asked a Blonde woman coming into the room.

The back portion of the bar where we were stationed was a few steps down from the rest of the bar, clearly another addition to the original building.

"I am."

"I'm Lori and this is my husband, Dan. He worked with your mom. I can't tell you how sorry we are and how much we are going to miss her."

"Thank you." Was that an appropriate response?

"We just loved your mom so much. I can't believe she's gone."

"Yeah, it was really unexpected. I'm not sure I've made it through the shock just yet."

"Do you mind me asking what happened?"

There's the million dollar question. More and more faces beginning to appear, how many of them coming to try and get information out of me?

"Terminal lung cancer."

"Did she know?"

"I'm not sure how long she knew, but she's known for at least a few months. She didn't want anyone to worry, so she didn't tell anyone right up until the end."

"Was she doing any sort of treatment?" Lori asked, looking genuinely concerned.

"She didn't. She also didn't want today to be sad. She always told me to make sure there was a celebration with beer and rock music when she went. So, I'm doing my best to honor her request."

"I think you've done a great job."

"Yeah, I'm just glad people are seeing the Facebook post. I don't have phone numbers for her friends and really want to make sure everyone has a chance to say goodbye."

"We let a few people know as soon as we saw the post."

"Brian," a hand touched my shoulder.

"Excuse me," I said, turning from Lori and her husband to an elderly woman who barely reached my shoulder.

"I don't know if you remember me."

"Of course I do," I said. How could I forget my mother's mother?

Rent (minus) Control

My mother's mother, my grandmother I suppose, has never been a presence in my life. She and Mom had a tumultuous history spanning decades. Giving her five children up for adoption, Mom was raised by her grandparents. Why she gave them all up I have no idea. It was a topic Mom refused to discuss and I didn't push. From stories other family members told me of their own experiences, it sounded like a lot of physical and emotional abuse. You can't blame someone for not wanting to discuss something so unpleasant.

Speaking to my grandmother for the first time as an adult, she shared her condolences. I believe she is saddened by the death, even if my Aunt, who was now outraged by her birth mother's presence, didn't agree. This day was about closure, and no one was allowed to be selfish and bring their family drama in the door. That is something to be dealt with tomorrow and at home.

Lucille, my grandmother, asked about my books and what I was doing with my life. Though Mom would probably roll over in her metaphorical grave at my cordial behavior, it was only appropriate, like I said, this isn't about me. We ended our conversation with me providing an address and phone number. Though I had no intention of staying in contact it would have been rude to refuse the request.

"Do you need anything?" Red asked, appearing out of nowhere, as the theme of the day seemed to be for everyone approaching me.

"A beer please. My face hurts from smiling."

R.B. Winters

"You got it."

"Oh my god," the voice was familiar.

Turning around I saw Mom's best friend Little Sherrie, or as we always joked, the short sawed-off circus midget. Well under five feet in height, Sherrie was a trucker like my mom, a loud, scratchy voice and a cheerful disposition. She was always laughing when I'd seen her in the past.

"How are you, B?"

"I'm ok. I'm so glad you could make it."

"Like hell I was going to miss this," Sherrie boomed, bringing me in for a hug. "You remember my daughter, Dusty."

"I do, it's nice to see you."

"You too. I'm so sorry about your mom."

Dusty, unlike her mom, was about my height, blonde, thin and a bit heavy on the makeup, but that's the way they do it in Utah.

"Thanks, it sucks, but what can you do about it."

"We need to get you a drink and cheers to your mom," said Sherrie.

"I like the way you think."

Being a truck driver, most of Mom's friends are as well. Each rolled in one after another, big, burly forty-something men crying on my shoulder and looking for some solace. Being so much like Mom, particularly our sharp tongues and quick wit it seemed like each of the visitors enjoyed sharing stories and getting a little piece of her from me. It was all I could provide them as there was no official funeral with time being pressed and me needing to get home.

The hours ticked by and eventually the crowd dispersed and it was me, my dad and stepmother, my siblings and Little Sherrie. We migrated to a table in the front of the bar to sit and drink. After several hours of running around and reminiscing this host was burned out. All I wanted was to relax for a moment.

Our time was short lived as a bouncer, or bartender, based on his large frame size he could be either or both, proclaimed,

"You all have to leave."

Dusty was being held up by the man ejecting us.

"What's wrong?" I asked, a good buzz finally kicking in after hours of being provided drinks from everyone who spoke to me.

"This one is falling all over herself," he said, handing Dusty off to Sherrie.

I'd not said anything, but earlier in the day when Dusty came from the bathroom she was rubbing her nose. I assumed she was doing coke, but who am I to judge, we each mourn in our own way.

Shuffling out the door, Sherrie and Dusty started arguing in the parking lot, my stepmom, Janet getting involved. Rachael and I walked away hand in hand.

"Why are you smiling?" Rachael asked.

"We were thrown out of my mom's wake. That's exactly how she'd want this night to end."

13. Driven

At long last, everything I never wanted to do was done and it was time to go home. The only thing remaining to be dealt with was Mom's car. A sporty black thing her ex, Cort, was dying to get his hands on. I'd been smart enough to bring it to Salt Lake where it would be out of reach.

It was shared, because of small town gossip, Cort wanted the car for his new fiancé. Like hell I was going to let that happen. You can't cheat, run out and then give the car of your ex to the woman you left her for. At least, you can't when I'm involved.

Knowing this is likely to be a battle I contacted the lawyer who took care of Mom and Cort's separation. Mark wasn't surprised by Cort's actions, he'd been a 'nightmare' during the breakup, dragging things out for more than a year. He agreed to help at a reasonable rate. I made my intentions clear: I would pay off the remaining balance of the car and Cort would then need to sign over the title and disappear from my life. Is that so much to ask?

Cort, refusing my offer, left me only one decision: Bring the car home to the East Coast and keep it hidden until he finally gives up on this frivolous pursuit. Not an ideal situation, but with Dennis and I together it was possible to drive across the country in a few days. It was also easier to transport the cat, which I decided to keep.

Saying goodbye to Rachael and family, the car was loaded up with the boxes of trinkets from Mom's apartment I wanted to keep, suitcases of dirty clothing from the last week and Goldie Hawn a.k.a. my new cat. The initial drive taking us up through Park City, past Red's house and into Wyoming was long, cold and boring as hell. Running out of things to discuss, Dennis and I began channel surfing the limited radio by hour three. That's when flashing red and blue lights appeared in the mirror.

"Fuck me," I said, pulling onto the shoulder.

Moments later an officer appeared at the passenger window, leaning down to speak.

"Where are we heading, gentlemen?"
"Home," I answered, trying to keep the attitude in check.
"Where's home?"
"New York."
"You're a long way out. What brings you here?" Asked the officer, who was semi attractive.
"My mom died. I've been hear taking care of her estate."

Rent (minus) Control

"Can I see your license and registration?"

Apparently my response was enough to stop the questioning. The officer now looking uncomfortable, wanting to get away from us as fast as I wanted to get away from him. Heading back to his patrol car, we sat for several minutes before the blonde stranger returned to Dennis' window.

"Because you were going more than twenty over the limit I can't let you go with a warning. But I did only mark you as being ten over the limit," he explained.

"Thanks," I said, reaching over Dennis to take the ticket and sign with the provided pen.

"Slow down and get home safe."

The officer returned to his car and we were once again on our way. As if this trip hadn't cost enough already, add another one-hundred and ten dollars to the total.

Stopping a hundred or so miles before Cheyenne, Wyoming it was time to eat. If only to stop the groaning pleas from my stomach. The only town we came across with food had a Thai place and a Burger King. As much as I love Burger King, a week of terrible eating and no exercise meant there was no way I was going to gorge on fatty fries and dripping burgers. So, Thai it is.

The two tables of patrons shot dagger looks as Dennis and I entered. What the hell is their problem?

"I hate small towns," I muttered to Dennis.

"Just the two of you?" A hostess asked, coming from the rear of the restaurant.

I was surprised to see a black employee in the middle of the whitest part of the country. She had to be from a foreign country.

"Can I get you something to drink?" Asked the hostess, sitting us at a table away from the other patrons.

She was definitely from outside the country, but I couldn't put my finger on the accent. A high pitched voice and a throaty accent made it possible for her to be from anywhere.

"Can I have an unsweetened iced tea?"
"We only have sweetened," she answered.
"Oh, then just a water," said Dennis.
"Water is fine," I added.

Catching my reflection in a mirror across the room, the heavy bags under my eyes made it evident the past week was leaving a lasting impact. Not only did I look like death, but I felt like it as well. Everything that had taken place was beginning to replay in my head as now there was time to think. Losing myself in the thoughts of wakes and sad faces, I jumped when a plate was placed in front of me.

'Thanks," I mumbled.

"Enjoy," said the host-waitress.

The food wasn't of the highest quality. Picking at the chicken, drenched in a brown sauce with the taste of a cheap glue. The white rice and broccoli being the only edible items.

Powering through the plate of awful, I was overjoyed when we left and Dennis volunteered to drive. My joy was short lived. Not only was the gooey meat on my plate unappetizing, but also bad, my stomach was about to explode.

"Can you stop at the next rest stop?" I asked, considering we may need to pull off on the side of the road.

"Sure, what's wrong?" Dennis asked.

"I think I may die. That food must have been bad." My stomach roared as the statement was made.

Playing the rest stop game for another hour, Dennis finally surrendered and we found a motel just before reaching Cheyenne. It wasn't much, including clean, but it had a toilet and meant I wouldn't be running in and out of another fly infested roadside shit hole. Pun, oh so fully, intended.

"Do you want to wait with the cat and I'll run in and book rooms?"

"Yeah, but hurry, I need a bathroom, *right now*."

Dennis ran inside, trying to be as quick as possible, me squirming in the seat as the cat decided now was the time she would come to the front seat and sit on my lap. Clearly she knew I was dying from the inside out and wanted to ensure the experience was that much worse. Pushing Goldie onto the floor I wiggled about, waiting for Dennis to return.

Two hours, a handful of pills from the front desk and I was almost human again, though I'd left most of myself spread across Wyoming. Ordering dinner from a chain pizza restaurant it seemed like a safe thing to eat. God bless corporate chains and health regulations.

With a rumbling, but full stomach, I climbed into bed after inspecting for bed bugs. One can never be too safe, not even in the middle of nowhere.

The morning beginning bright and early, I drove us for the first hundred miles, until I spotted a truck stop with a sign for Starbucks. Like a Born-Again Christian, I saw my salvation.

"Do you want anything?" I asked Dennis, pulling up to the gas pump so he could refuel the car while I grabbed delicious coffee.

"No, I'm fine."

"Ok, here are the keys," I said, sitting them on the console between us.

Heading inside I found the world's smallest and busiest Starbucks. One kid, running the register and the espresso machine. Nine people ahead of me in line. Annoyed, I waited my turn, giving my order before getting to wait in line a second time as the kid attempted to fill all the orders ahead of mine.

Knowing it wasn't his fault the line appeared all at once, or that the manager only scheduled one person, I did my best to remain calm and wait for the latte. As my order came up, Dennis entered the building.

"Did you change your mind?"

"No. We have a problem?" Dennis said.

"What kind of problem?" I asked. What could have possibly gone wrong in the last ten minutes?

"The cat locked us out of the car?"

"Excuse me?" Since when can cats lock car doors?

"The lock buttons are on the center arm rest and she walked over it. I didn't realize you left the keys with me until I tried getting inside."

"Are you kidding me?" I asked, following Dennis to the car.

There on the seat sat Goldie Hawn, next to her the car keys. Then I noticed what I had left in the cup holder.

"Oh my god, I left my phone inside. Fuck me."

"It's ok. I've already called a lock smith."

"How? Your phone's right next to mine."

"The girl in the station let me use the phone."

"This day is off to a great fucking start."

Pissed at the cat and wanting to throttle her I took comfort that I at least had coffee to make me feel better. That was until the locksmith pulled up to the car. A van covered in a wrap to look like camouflage.

"Are you kidding me?"

The locksmith stepped out of the van. A gray beard down to his waist, a black bandana and chaps.

"Wow, they sent a Duck Dynasty cast member to help us."

Dennis spoke to the locksmith as I formed rude opinions of him from a distance. I didn't want to watch him get the door open, if he scratched the car's paint Mom would surely rise from the dead and haunt me for all of eternity. It took a good twenty minutes, but the soon to be television star opened the car at a cost of only sixty dollars. A country style bargain.

Learning a valuable lesson, I kept a tight hold on the car keys each time we exited the car for the remainder of the trip. It took another day and a half, but we made the long drive to New York. Fortunately, aside from bad Thai food and a stint of kitty drama the drive was event free and nothing but long, boring stretches of road.

14. Friends

The eight tiny boxes in the backseat of the car took no time to unload. Made faster with the help of Dimitri and Larry. Waiting in my apartment when we arrived, I was never more glad to have given someone a spare key. Dennis headed off to deal with his hotel room and get some rest before retrieving his own car from the airport.

"We got Miss. Goldie Hawn a new bed," Larry said, pointing out a plush kitty bed in my bedroom below one of the lengthy windows.

"Very nice, she's definitely living the high life. A week ago she was a stray, this week she's a city kitty."

"She's adorable," Dimitri added.

"Yeah, but I think I want to change her name. If I wasn't gay enough, having a cat named, Goldie Hawn, is really going to put me over the top."

"You could call her Goldie or GH," Larry suggested.

"That's true."

"You haven't seen the best part. We decided to get you a belated housewarming present."

"Wine?" I asked, really wanting it to be wine.

"We brought that too, but it's not the present. We installed dimmers in the bedroom and bathroom."

Sticking my head into the bathroom, on the wall where once was a simple on and off switch, I discovered a new round dial. Giving it a turn the lights slowly began to burn amber, amplifying with the turn to reach a white glow.

"You'll be glad to have them when you get up in the middle of the night," Dimitri said.

"You have no idea. I get up three or four times every night and leave them off because the light is so blinding bright. Thank you guys, this is awesome."

The little things people do make a significant impact. There's little anyone can do for you after a situation like I've experienced, but it's comforting to know there are people around who care.

Dimitri opened the wine, pouring three glasses. A toast to nothing specific, but a toast nonetheless.

"How did everything go?" Larry asked, being sensitive to the situation, unsure how emotional I would be on the topic.

"Things went better than expected. I did realize my family is full of vultures, only showing up to haul things off from my mom's place."

"*Really?* That's tacky."

"I guess it shouldn't be a surprise. But the wake was fun. We drank and ended up getting thrown out of the bar."

"How'd that happen?" Dimitri asked, sipping at his glass of wine.

"My mom's, best friend's, daughter was in the bathroom doing coke. The bartender threw us out when she was falling down at the bar."

"That's fucked up."

"It was kind of the perfect end to a crazy day. I should have asked her if she had extra, I'm sure coke is way cheaper in Utah."

I shared the other antics of the week, including the cat locking the car doors. I'm still mad at her for that incident, little bitch.

"Can I ask what happened to your mom exactly?" Dimitri prodded, still treading lightly.

"Officially, I'm leaving the story at lung cancer. Which she did have and I believe was a huge motivator in her decision."

"So, she knew she had cancer?" Larry asked.

"I've been constructing a timeline in my head and when she started talking about death related things. At the time I just thought she was being morbid, but it started somewhere around six months ago. And then last week."

I held two fingers to my head and made the motion of pulling a trigger. The words were not yet comfortable on my tongue and purging them from my body was proving difficult. Even contemplating them through gesture was causing tears to rise.

"I hate that she didn't tell me."

"I'm sure she didn't want you to worry," Dimitri assured.

"I know, but I'd rather have known so we could have spent the last few months together."

"Maybe we should change the subject," suggested Larry.

"Yes, please," I said, sniffling into my wine.

We spent time chatting about nothing in particular before my friends made for the train to Astoria. They'd been kind to stay as late as they did considering both had to work in the morning. Technically, I needed to work in the morning, but work was feeling less important than ever.

After their departure my phone buzzed. *Back in the City?* Leo had incredible timing. We hadn't communicated since the flight to Utah. Now was as good a time as any. *I'm home.* In no time, Leo was at my place. As the buzzer chimed I held down the button to release the door. Opening it after a gentle knock, I was very much surprised by the sight.

Leo stood in the doorway with a dozen pink roses.

"Hi," I said.

"Hi," Leo kissed my cheek, handing over the flowers.

"Thanks."

The last time a guy gave me flowers was more than a decade before this moment. A giant, gaudy mess of flowers delivered to my work. Not only was I mortified upon their arrival but it was the end of the relationship. Ironically, my mother had kept the flowers sent to me originally, and now I was getting flowers because of her. Maybe it's more coincidental than ironic, but to me it will be as such.

"How are you doing?" Leo asked, sitting at the bar stool on the small strip of counter that distinguished the kitchen from the rest of the apartment.

"Ok, I guess. I'm not sure there's a right answer."

"I grabbed some food, want any?"

"I'm fine. Would you like a glass of wine? I even have white for a change." I suggested, knowing Leo preferred white wine to red.

"No thanks."

Refilling my glass, I leaned against the fridge across from the man in my apartment. His visit was a surprise. The idea of a good sexual encounter was appealing and perhaps just the thing to refocus a mind gone wild.

"When did you get back?"

"Tonight actually."

"Nice. How are you really doing?"

Sometimes you wonder if people can see through the facade to what's really going on, or if they're just asking the obligatory questions.

"Honestly?"

"Yeah."

"I feel like I'm emotionally clogged. I should be crying nonstop, but I keep swallowing my tears and half the time I'm not even sure there are any left in there."

"Everyone grieves different. Just let it happen."

"I guess."

Leo finished eating and we talked about my new pet. Me fearing the fur that would soon overtake everything, Leo recommending I invest in a roller. Planning ahead, Leo bought a toothbrush along with the flowers, excusing himself to rinse away the takeout.

Now late in the night, we climbed into my bed. Leo was officially the first person to spend the night in this apartment with me. I leaned into him, his arm coming over my side.

"This is new."

"What do you mean?" I asked, my hand moving under the pillow as I made myself comfortable.

"You never try to cuddle with me."

I didn't answer. He was right, I never attempted to cuddle. Why was I doing so now?

15. Time

Seven weeks of back and forth between two lawyers, myself and Cort, we finally came to an agreement. Mom's car was signed over to me with the understanding I would immediately pay the outstanding loan balance off in full. The lawyer cited the triumph as coming from his excellent negotiation skills. I believe it's because I made it very clear in the last conversation I would happily fight Cort over the car until the day he dies. I'm younger, technically I should outlive him.

The car didn't mean anything to me. Aside from wanting to carry out Mom's last wishes to her liking, there's nothing I could do with a car. My street really has no parking and the traffic coming off the Queensboro Bridge is so intense during rush hour, any car parked on the street is likely to be rammed by aggravated drivers.

All this time I'd been storing the car at my boss and friend, Dennis', home in Baltimore. This had two benefits. One: I knew the car was safe. Two: If Cort hadn't decided to give up or sent someone to retrieve the car, the odds of him finding it were fairly slim.

With the car already in Baltimore it was worth a train ride to sell it to CarMax. It was fortune the car was no longer in production and in high demand. Thank god, Mom had good taste. Selling it was quick and painless, but a little sad. I waited until I had to turn the keys over to take the green, beaded dragonfly off of the rearview mirror. It had hung in Mom's last two cars and it was a way of keeping her memory there. Now the dragonfly had to come home with me.

The salesgirl was sweet. She didn't know why I was selling the car and didn't directly ask. Filling out the paperwork, getting my signature and handing me the Utah license plates, she sent me on my way.

"That was less horrible than I imagined," I said, tucking the license plates inside my computer case and hanging it off my shoulder.

"CarMax is great. They always make it easy. I sell all my cars here," said Dennis. "What time it your train?"

Checking the time on my phone,

"I have about three hours before I need to be at Penn Station."

"Should we grab a drink downtown while we wait?"

"Yes, please. A big glass of wine would be great right now."

Dennis drove us to The Owl Bar located inside the Belvedere Hotel. Entering the historic building we were greeted by a hallway decorated in photos. Presidents, sports figures and famous people from the last century lived inside the frames of all sizes. They looked out at us with their blaring smiles, holding on forever to a moment that had long slipped into the past.

The space making up the bar was unique in its own right. The mahogany bar, stools and adjacent tables all from a period before I'd ever come to know this world. Stained glass windows hung well above the point for viewers to look in or out. Sunlight coming through the multi-colored glass and illuminating the few heads sitting along the bar. Perched above the bottles of whiskey and vodka was a plastic owl, tied to an aging piece of wood that was probably once a work of art. Now it looked like a broken fragment sticking from the wall, ready to give splinters to anyone trying to remove the bird perched under layers of dust.

"This is a cool bar," I said as we settled on a wobbly table in the corner.

"I haven't been here in a while, but it's a decent place to throw back a drink."

"I like it."

"Hey guys, can I get you something to drink?" A blonde waitress appeared, pulling a pad and pen from her deep pockets.

"Can I get a glass of the house red, please?" I asked.

"Sure. And for you?"

"I'll have the same."

Once drinks arrived and we were a few sips in, Dennis asked,

"Is this the last thing?"

"The last Mom thing?" I asked, making sure this wasn't the beginning of an intervention. No one can take away my wine.

"Yeah, I mean the car. Is this the last thing you had to take care of?"

"It was. It's sort of a relief, it's finally all over. At the same time I'm a little sad it's all over, because it means, *it's over.* You know?"

"It's hard, but it's important to start moving on."

"True. I don't want to become one of those people you see on TV who suddenly have twenty cats and forty years of newspapers stacked in their studio apartment."

Dennis raised his glass.

"A toast to remaining sane," he said.

"As sane as any of us will ever be," I added, clinking our glasses. "Give me your advice." I said, placing my glass on the table and giving it a gentle swirl, the crimson liquid lapping at the edges. "After I pay off all the credit cards I've charged up during this process there will be a little money left. My mom said to split it between Jeremy and myself, but I feel like I should also give my sister a portion. What would you do?"

"You could keep it. Usually the person that closes out an estate charges a fee and you've gone way beyond thorough."

"I don't really want any of the money. If I spent it on something for me I'd always be forced to think about where it came from."

"You're thinking you want to split it with your siblings?"

"That's the problem. My brother never works and spends his time sucking his friends dry, one couch at a time. I don't want to just hand him a bunch of money that will be blown on booze. And my sister, it would be fine to give her a portion, I guess."

"What about giving them an experience?"

"What do you mean?" I asked, hailing the waitress for another glass of wine, mine having miraculously run dry.

"Rather than giving them each a check, do something like fly them to New York."

"That could work for my sister, but with my brother it won't. I'm not really interested in him being in my life. He'll just start calling me for handouts like he did with our mom."

"Then give him a check and call it good."

There wasn't a simple answer to the question. What was the right thing to do with the money? So far I'd followed all the directions provided. Technically, the directions said to split any leftover cash between Jeremy and myself, but it felt wrong to leave Jami out. She and Mom weren't close and they fought any time they were in the same room, but she's still her daughter.

"Maybe I will ask my sister if she and her kids want to come out for a visit. I could use her share and mine to cover the flights and have a little spending cash on hand when they arrive."

"That's a good idea. That way you will give them something they can always remember," said Dennis.

"My brother can just have the check. It's probably not the smartest thing, but it's what my mom would have wanted me to do. I think."

"Well, you can't control what he does with the money. All you can do is hope he puts it to good use."

"I hope he doesn't blow it all on a hooker or at a bar, but we can play a game of *don't ask, don't tell* and I'll play ignorant."

Dennis drove me up the street to Penn Station where I boarded the Amtrak headed for New York. Calling Jami once I was settled in the cafe car.

"Hello?"

"Hey, it's B. How are you?"

"Hey, B. I'm good, just finishing my lunch break. What are you up to?"

"On the train heading home. I sold mom's car today." My comment struck silence. "Anyway, I wanted to ask you if you'd be interested in coming to visit."

"I can't afford to come out there right now."

"Well, there's a little money left from selling the car. I thought I could combine your portion and mine to pay for plane tickets for you and the kids. What do you think?"

"That could be fun. I haven't been to New York since I was little and my dad was living out there."

Opening my laptop I searched the JetBlue homepage for tickets in July. Being two months away I'd expect lower prices, though none were to be found. But that's what happens when summer arrives and everybody is trying to get away.

"There are some decent tickets for the Fourth of July."

"That won't work. The kids are going to Vegas to visit Gary."

Gary had a long history with our family. When I was ten he dated my mom. And through a series of events, none of which have ever made sense, he ended up moving to Las Vegas and becoming Jami's, father's roommate. They were roommates until Jami's dad went to prison five years ago. Gary lost her dad's house to the bank from what I heard. The idea that they have any contact is baffling to me.

"What about the weekend of July twenty-fourth?" I asked, scanning the website for flights with three vacant seats.

"That might work. I'll need to ask my boss, but as long as she's ok with it, I'm in."

"Cool. Well, I'll book the tickets and if anything changes let me know. We can change the dates if we need to."

"Okay. Let me let you go, I need to get back inside."

"Talk to you later."

Hanging up the phone, I purchased the tickets for Jami and her two kids. It was several weeks away but I was excited by the idea of them coming to see me.

16. Fourth

Seeing as I love to write about my shallow thoughts one would think getting back to writing would be the first order of business. Putting pen to paper, or in this case, fingers to keyboard, was proving incredibly difficult. Every time I attempted to start a new blog or even work on a chapter, the lines quickly became depressing and dark. Not the brooding, sexy dark that comes with a story about vampires and pornographic sex, but the kind of dark that comes when you have to admit to yourself certain feelings are real.

Doing my best to skip over my feelings and any grief, I attempted to shove all feelings related to Mom into the pit of my stomach where they could properly fester and reemerge as an ulcer. The plan didn't work as well as initially expected. Sometimes while out with friends, or at the end of a sad movie, even in the middle of a drunken conversation I was bursting into tears. All the feelings forced into my stomach were clawing their way out through my eyes. Something that was difficult to hide.

As the Fourth of July approached and a little time was between me, my feelings and all the craziness that began the year, it was beginning to feel as though things might returning to normal. Dimitri was hosting a barbecue and it was the perfect opportunity to get out of my head and into the present.

With two bottles of wine in hand I made my way to Queens.

"You don't have to touch me, I'm all sweaty," I said, Dimitri opening the door to his home.

"Is it that hot?"

"No, I just walk too fast. Am I the first one here?"

"Larry's downstairs."

"Hooray!"

For the last two weeks I've not seen much of my friends. Their dating lives have been getting in the way of our wine time. As far as dating, I was on an unofficial break. It was likely that I'd have one or two drinks, they might ask about my family and then I'd be crying in their lap, or worse, explaining why I'm *okay* with everything. Either way, no one wants to hear that shit and I don't want to be responsible for sharing.

"Hey," I greeted Larry as I came down the spiral wooden steps.

"Hey, how are you?"

"Good. What are these?"

"I made Jell-O shots."

"Oh my god, I love you like a drag queen right now."

"This was my first attempt, but I figure it can't be that hard. I tested the first batch out last night."

"How were they?" I asked, nearly overcome by a desire to start shoveling the tiny cups of orange into my mouth.

"I was shit face drunk."

"So, good?"

"Try one." Larry offered one of the thimble size cups full of toxic delicious.

Downing the vodka drenched gelatin I was pleasantly surprised. Unlike the shots that are sold by the drag queens at nearly every gay bar in the city on weekends, these are actually a jiggly gel, tasting of orange and not cheap vodka.

"I want ten of these in my mouth now."

"They're good, right?"

"Where'd you get the recipe?"

"I pulled it off the Internet. They're really easy. I'm going to start making them for all the parties."

"If I were you, I would sit home and eat them all."

"I did have a big bowl leftover, so I put it in the fridge. I'm going to binge watch Netflix tonight and eat it by the spoonful," Larry confessed.

"Every part of that statement makes me happy."

Dimitri appeared after we finished tasting another round of orange shots. He had in tow a tall, plump ginger.

"Ryan, this is Patrick."

I extended a hand. As we shook,

"We've met," Patrick said.
"Have we?"
"Yeah a few weeks back. I was here with my boyfriend."
"Oh, right, you're dating the French guy."

My realization apparently struck a cord, Patrick withdrawing his hand, returning his attention to Dimitri as they walked to the backyard where the barbecue was ready to be prepped.

"I vaguely remember this guy," I said to Larry, hoping he could fill in the mental gap.

"That's the guy Dimitri dated years ago. Back then he was a skinny ginger."

"That makes more sense. I was going to ask when Dimitri became interested in the plus size gays."

Our heads turned as footsteps came from the stairs behind us.

"Hey, guys."

Scott and Erika appeared from the staircase of mysteries. They were one of two straight couples I'd been introduced to in the past year by Larry and Dimitri. I was a big fan, and not only because after a few drinks Scott would let me play with his girlfriend's boobs, but it definitely didn't hurt the situation.

"Hey, straight kids!" I was feeling a buzz off two Jell-O shots. Either my tolerance was down or they were incredibly strong.

"How are you?" Erika asked.

We exchanged hugs and pleasantries before my attention shifted to Erika's shorts.

"I love that you're wearing rape shorts."

"Are they bad?" she asked.

"No, they're amazing. Short enough to look ghetto and just long enough to hide your business."

We laughed as Dimitri returned, pouring a round of drinks for the growing group. As an excellent host and bartender, Dimitri prevented glasses from running dry. This meant as an attendee to one of his gatherings, assuming you're not religious or a reformed alcoholic, you are guaranteed to have a good time.

It wasn't long before the party was moving outside around a glass table. My fear: Mosquitos. Something about my blood was attractive to the little bastards. Sit me outside for more than ten minutes and I was sure to be consumed. This means I am constantly shifting around in my seat and rubbing my exposed skin. If you didn't know what I was doing it probably looked as though I was so turned on by myself that it was impossible to hide. That, or it looked like I had a horrible meth addiction.

Rent (minus) Control

As food began to grill, Cards Against Humanity played amongst our group. As the game's slogan claims, this is a 'card game for horrible people.' For a group such as this it was the perfect game, made better as everyone in attendance is a perverted extrovert.

Somewhere between the second round of the game and the fourth glass of wine, I needed to use the bathroom. Excusing myself and slinking back inside the house I made a pit stop. While washing my hands and glaring into the mirror, those tricky gears inside my head began to grind.

"Fuck me." I knew what was about to happen.

Stumbling back into the kitchen, I found my phone plugged into the wall behind the table. Pulling the cord from the USB socket and shoving it in a pocket, I picked my keys and wallet up from the table. The phone started to vibrate as I hauled myself up the steps and out the door. My friend, Brittany, from Baltimore was calling.

"Hello."

"Hey, what are you doing?"

"Just walked out of a party. You?" God, walking is so hard. Why does Dimitri live so far from the train?

"Pre-gaming before I meet friends. What party are you leaving?"

"My friend is having a thing at his place in Queens. I feel some crazy coming on, so I snuck out. I figure these guys have had enough of my mommy drama. I don't want to ruin their day by getting sad."

"What's going on?"

Thank the devil for the existence of alcohol, if not for being pumped full of it I'd likely give a canned answer to mask any actual emotion that made me appear remotely human.

"I feel like I'm going crazy."

"How so?" Brit asked, sounding sympathetic.

"This whole death thing. Everything hit so fast and I marched in, cleaned up the mess with my brave face, now it's all this time later and it feels like I missed my chance to grieve."

"Everyone grieves differently."

"But it's like I'm clogged. There was the random crying thing for a while, but now I just feel like throwing myself off the fire escape."

"Let's not do that...unless we jump together."

"Deal."

"You just need time to process," Brit advised.

"If I were someone listening to me, my advice to them would be to get over it and move on. I'm having real difficulty following my own advice."

"We're all good at giving advice, but can any of us actually take it?"

"Fair enough, I guess. It's fine, I just need to go home and get out of my head. It's probably the worst place for me to be right now."

"Well, if you want to talk or drunk text me later, I'm around."

"You'll be hearing from me. That's a promise."

Hanging up, the phone back in my pocket, the train could be heard rumbling over the tracks above. Pulling it together, I bolted, taking the steps two at a time, through the turnstile, out of breath I passed inside the car as the doors made their closing ding, sliding shut.

Once home I did the best thing I could think. Grabbing a six pack of beer, I downed three, wrapping a fourth in a paper bag. Walking the two avenues to the East River Walkway, crowds had started forming in anticipation of fireworks. Not tall enough to see over the heads, and drunk enough to not worry about safety, I climbed beer in hand up the chain-link fence and atop the concrete storage shed that had no known purpose. Well, I'm sure it has some purpose, but who the hell knows what it's for.

Plopping on the edge, legs dangling over the East River, in the far distance fireworks could be seen. Those to the south bursting over the Brooklyn Bridge and others in the East somewhere in Queens. This wasn't the evening I'd planned, turning more dramatic than intended by my random party departure. But being alone, with a crowd of strangers was exactly what I needed in this moment.

17. Arrival

The weeks following my mini breakdown were met with forgiving friends. Though I think it was the last time I can use the mommy card as an excuse for bad behavior, things have truly began to calm. No longer do I catch myself thinking, *'I should call mom.'* I'm also no longer catching myself waiting for the phone to ring with calls that will never come.

Dennis suggested calling Mom's phone when I get the urge to talk to her and leaving voicemails. His thought is that in time I could turn them into an interesting book. The idea is good, but my mission to ensure every bill was paid and account closed meant the phone was off, but the actual device is in my possession...be that for better or worse.

My head was back on a level playing field just in time for my sister's visit. Seeing as she and her kids are on the redeye from Salt Lake City, I pulled myself out of bed just after four in the morning to grab a ZipCar. It was either this or try to explain to them how you get from JFK to my apartment in a cab. Either way the ZipCar is less money and far less stress.

With my earbuds in, I blasted the best of Britney Spears as the phone explained to me how to drive to JFK. Having not been behind the wheel for a while, it was a welcome surprise to find the early morning streets free of cars. Too bad the return visit wouldn't be the same. Arriving only five minutes late, I pulled up to the curb, my sister and the kids sitting patiently on a bench with their bags.

Popping the trunk after realizing the button was on the center console, everyone loaded their bags and then piled into the four-door sedan.

"Hi, Uncle Brian," said my nephew Brian.

I may have ditched the name Brian along with my Utah roots, but there's an interesting backstory to my potential namesake. When my sister was pregnant with Brian, just before her seventeenth birthday, she told me she wanted to name him after me. At the time I was only eleven, not thinking much more than it would be cool to have someone named after me I encouraged the decision. A year or so later when I was visiting my sister at her home in Las Vegas, her then husband Ernesto and I took a walk to a nearby gas station for him to buy Jami cigarettes.

It was late in the evening and we'd had a long day. The two of them trying to entertain me on this weekend visit. As Ernesto and I walked he brought up the topic of his new son. He was compelled to make sure I knew he wasn't actually named after me, but a fellow drug dealer he knew who was recently killed. He continued to explain he was only letting Jami think the baby was named after me so she wouldn't object to the name. I didn't have a response. What can you say to something like that? He should have kept this information to himself, but there it was, forever in my head. Ernesto asked me to not tell my sister, and I never have.

"How was your flight?" I asked, Jami climbing into the front passenger seat, both kids buckling into the back.

"Not bad. Poor Brian had me sleeping on one shoulder and Desiree sleeping on the other."

"Better than sleeping on a stranger," I said, trying to navigate into the moving traffic exiting the airport.

"Uncle Brian, do you have a driver's license?" Desiree asked.

"I do, but I never have to use it. Which is safer for everyone."

With traffic beginning to jam up the expressway I did my best to make the car ride entertaining and educational. As Manhattan came into view, pointing out the Empire State Building, the Chrysler Building and of course, World Trade Center One, or the Freedom Tower. It's hard to keep track of what they're calling it these days.

"Do you guys want to take a nap when we get to the apartment or do you want to head out and start seeing things?" I asked, looking in the rearview mirror to gauge the reaction.

Rent (minus) Control

Brian had called the day after I booked the plane tickets to thank me. I explained the trip was only possible because of his grandmother's death, trying to do so in the least morbid way possible. As I explained to Jami, I wanted this trip to be one good memory she could associate with our mother. Knowing they spent the last decade fighting and having no real resolution had to be weighing on her.

Desiree took the opposite approach of Brian, she complained about having to come on the trip. Not wanting to leave her boyfriend. Jami told me this over the phone, to which I responded by telling her, *'I don't want to hear about teenage love. They'll break up in a month and she'll be in love with someone new in two. Let me know when she's twenty-five, broken and ready to talk.'* Jami laughed, but I was serious when I told her the kids didn't have to come if they were opposed. We could cash in their tickets and use the money to have a great time. She declined and insisted they would have fun, so here we are.

Before beginning what I hoped would be an entertaining day of sightseeing, we stopped by the Ritz Diner for breakfast, it was only seven in the morning. The Russian waitress was quick, Brian hesitating to put in his drink order and missing the opportunity twice. It's always interesting to see someone in New York for the first time. Some people love the pace, others find it stressful and overwhelming.

With bellies full, I led our group to Starbucks for mobile coffee and then onto the train, our first stop, the Brooklyn Bridge. The bridge was symbolic for me, having walked over it on every visit Mom made to New York from the beginning. The thought was to continue the tradition and share it with Jami. I didn't go into detail with Jami on the significance of the bridge, other than to tell her I always walked it with anyone who came to visit.

Walking the aging wooden planks, the cool morning air flowed over the bridge, a comfortable temperature and the perfect day to be wandering. Brian and I chatted, Jami walking behind and Desiree moping farther back.

"Let's take a picture. If we do it here you can get the tower of the bridge in," I said, pulling out my phone to snap a few photos.

Jami put her arm around Brian, Desiree being the typical teen and pulling away.

"Pretend you're happy," I prodded in an effort to at least get one of them to smile.

"You'll have to send me copies," Jami said.

"I'll text them to you now."

We walked the remaining length of the bridge in virtual silence. I'd put in some effort to make things light and entertaining, but it was becoming exhausting and clearly the effort was being wasted.

"Where are we going?" Desiree asked, her long, black sleeves disguising her as an emo.

"We're going to stop by the park where I spread my mom's ashes. I told your mom I'd show her."

I recognized after saying the words I should have said *your grandma*' but they were never close. Aside from living with Mom for a very short time, the kids had nothing but bad feelings for her due to the conflict she and Jami perpetuated.

"So, this is the tree."

We stood in Brooklyn Bridge Park. The place was peaceful, a few random pedestrians walking dogs, the antique carousel encased in glass not yet open and the ferry pulling away from its dock. This was the place I spread the ashes. It was directly below the bridge and had a perfect view of Manhattan.

Everyone stood silently looking around without focus.

"I thought you'd want to see it," I said, plucking a leaf from the tree.

The awkward intensity was beginning to rise as no one said a word, so it seemed like a change of scenery was best. Taking the crew back to the train, we made our way downtown to Battery Park. This was my favorite place in the city. Once you passed the Trade Center buildings and make it to the waterfront it is a night and day difference. The noise of the city fades away, people on leisurely strolls, boats drifting by, this was the most peaceful place in all of Manhattan.

Sitting on a bench beside the pier, we joked about making the ten foot plunge into the water. Attempting to share my nerdy fun facts, I pointed out the Colgate clock, which happened to be in front of a building where I once met a date's best lady friend. She was amazing and a big drunk. If there wasn't a bottle of Jameson in her hand you knew something was wrong. I learned this all in the length of a single night.

"Should we walk and find somewhere to have a drink? I feel like it's time for a Bloody Mary?"

"Sure," Jami said, putting out her cigarette and following my lead.

To my surprise when we met the place where once you had to go around massive walls, there was open space. The Trade Center Plaza was now open to the public and people freely roamed the space.

"This is crazy. The last time I was down here you had to have tickets to see the fountains and go through ten layers of security." I was stunned to see all the security stripped away and the space functioning like any other. "Let's take another photo."

Forcing Jami and the kids together in front of the massive black fountain, water fading into the depths behind, I snapped a few shots.

"Let's take one of me and you," Jami said.

I handed my phone to Brian, tapping at the screen he captured the first photo of Jami and I in more than a decade. It had been so long since we'd been in any sort of photo appropriate setting I couldn't tell you exactly when or where the last photo took place.

Leaving the masses and finding an upscale pub nearby, we paused for a rest and a drink. Jami and I ordered beers, the kids getting cola. A plate of nachos and conversation and it really felt as though things were moving in the right direction. After six long hours we were beginning to connect.

18. Departure

Two beers and it was clear Jami and the kids needed a nap before we went out for the evening. The plan was for the kids to stay home and order a pizza, while I showed Jami a good time. We were only back in the apartment for a few minutes and both kids had passed out, one on the sofa, the other on the floor. Jami took a quick shower, but even she couldn't stay awake, falling asleep next to Desiree on the sofa while I made dinner.

The smell of food, and a tap on the shoulder, was enough to rouse Jami back to the land of consciousness. Nothing glamorous, pasta and pre-made sauce from a jar. Two stools stood behind the pint size wall that broke the kitchen off from the rest of the apartment. If this was a single family home and the wall was more than three inches thick it would probably be referred to as a bar. I have no idea what to call the thing.

Grabbing a round of beers from the fridge, we made our way to the roof. The sun was beginning to set, taking with it the heat of the day. Still, the light was such that you could comfortably gaze off at the buildings in the distance, squint free.

"I think Desiree will eventually come around and be the one to like New York," I declared.

Desiree expressed earlier in the day she didn't know how anyone could live in New York. She played the common outsider complaint of *'needing a car'* which is comical seeing as she doesn't have a license and won't for at least another year. I didn't combat the comment or any of her other gripes about the city, knowing she, like so many others, didn't yet understand the magic of living in a big city, particularly living in New York.

"You think?" Jami asked, popping the caps off our beers.

"If she's putting all of this effort into looking and being different, she's never going to thrive in Utah."

"I guess, I just don't think I could live here."

"It's not so bad, you just need to adjust."

"I can't even tell which way we're walking half the time."

"It took me a while. I would come out of the subway when I first moved here, think I was going the right way, and two avenues later realize everything was backwards."

"Maybe she'll change her mind, but I can't see it happening."

There's nothing wrong with growing up in Utah. It's full of family values and annoying religious people who are unnaturally pleasant. As long as you remain in the box of acceptable behavior you'll be fine. Go outside the box and no one will directly engage or confront you, but you'll become an outsider who is being prayed for on Sundays and always have to deal with whispers behind your back. That's a lifestyle I found intolerable. If you despise someone or something with such passion, please do yourself a favor and confront the issue rather than gossiping amongst your single minded peers.

"*Hey!* How'd you guys get in?" I stood, beer in hand, to greet Dimitri and Larry who had come from the lock-free silver door which granted access to the roof.

"We followed some girl in. Hope you don't mind," Larry said, hugging me over the black railing intended to keep people, like me, from getting too near the edge of the building.

Where Jami and I positioned ourselves was technically out of bounds. Well, all of the roof is out of bounds. Apparently if you're caught up here it's grounds for instant eviction. Considering there are five vacant apartments in the building at the moment it's a safe assumption no one will be pushing me out the front door.

"Of course not. You saved me a trip down to hit the buzzer."

"And we brought wine," Dimitri said, extracting from a slender black sack a bottle of red deliciousness.

Polishing off the bottle of wine and the remaining beers in the fridge, it was time to take Jami out and show her all New

York City has to offer. Showing my nephew how to use the food app on the iPad and asking them to keep the tab under fifty bucks, we set out for Hell's Kitchen. Seeing as Jami wasn't on the hunt for a man we had the advantage of skipping the straight bars and getting right to the gay fun.

Therapy was the first stop. Offering a relaxed and dimly lit atmosphere, this bar was perfect for people watching and small groups. Unfortunately the crowd began to grow with the volume of music. This pushed our posse out the door and farther West. But not before one stop.

"We have to stop by Baby's," I said, walking arm-in-arm with Jami.

Dimitri and Larry were only a few steps behind, everyone laughing over something that was said ten minutes earlier.

"Who's Baby?" Jami asked. "Can we get cigarettes?"

"Sure, we'll stop in the bodega up here," I said, pointing a drunken finger towards a light in the distance. "Baby's my dealer."

"You do drugs?" Jami's tone was disapproving, I probably shouldn't be telling her the details of what goes on behind the scenes.

"Now and then. Usually when there's a special occasion."

"You better be careful and not get addicted to something."

"I look at it like this. I can't afford a drug habit and as long as I go to work, pay my bills and don't hurt anyone it's fine."

My explanation didn't appear to comfort Jami's mind. Her face remained contorted which I found rather perplexing. Her ex-husband was a drug dealer. In fact, he was in prison at this very moment for getting busted selling cocaine. I find it nearly impossible to believe in their long and dramatic history together that drugs weren't consumed by the both at least once.

Jami purchased her cigarettes from the Pakistani clerk as I withdrew money from the ATM. Baby was conveniently located in the center of all things gay, which is not only practical but also good business sense from her standpoint. One block, three text messages and we were at the steps of Baby's building.

"You can wait out here if you like," I said, knowing Larry and Dimitri would wait outside.

"It's fine, I'll go in with you," Jami replied.

Once inside Baby's apartment, which by the way is three times the size of mine, too bad it's on the ground floor otherwise I'd be asking to move into the spare bedroom, we completed our transaction. But not before I explained who the random female on my arm was.

"Oh my god, I loved your mother," Baby said, her heavy New York accent smothering every syllable. "She was such a sweetheart. She told me once if my mom didn't want me, she'd take me."

Seeing the distain on Jami's face I squashed the conversation, rushing us out the door. Baby loved my mom. Baby met her one time five years ago and it left such an impression that she brings Mom up any time we see one another. You would think a single memory would fade away, but it's stronger than ever, and probably a bad time to share the news of her passing. Avoiding reality, I thanked Baby, gave her a hug and we were again on our way.

"Can we go dance?" Jami asked.

"Um, always," I replied. "How about Ritz?" I put the question out to the group.

With a consensus on which bar to dance at we strolled over to The Ritz. This was one of those bars that's a million degrees inside, with partially dressed people, everyone is dancing with, on or near someone. Two levels, both with bars, bathrooms and dance floors. It doesn't get much better.

We danced. And danced. And drank. Sweaty, hot and probably more intoxicated than was acceptable when going home to two teenagers, it was time to get out of this place. Exiting being no small chore as it required forcing yourself between bodies the entire length of the bar to escape into the cool evening air. The front patio was filled with smokers. Though I didn't smoke, every time I exited this bar and the smell wafted against me, I smiled. Who knows why, it's just one of those strange habits you create over time.

"I think I dropped my cigarettes," Jamie said, plopping down on the stoop next door to the bar.

"I'll go look for them. Probably won't find them, but I can look," I said. "Come with me." I tugged on Larry's arm.

Back in the bar we did a quick pass to search for the smokes among the many pairs of feet. That was until an amazing song came on and we were forced to take a dance break. Luck was on our side and Larry found cigarettes on the floor. They weren't Jami's but they would be in a minute.

"Here we found your cigarettes." I held out the crinkled pack as we returned to the stoop.

Something was wrong, Jami had tears in her eyes and a look on her face.

"What?" I asked, confused. Did I miss something?

"Fuck you." Jami pulled the cigarettes from my outstretched hand.

"You guys should get a cab and go."

"You two can take the first one," Dimitri replied.

"No, you'll want to go first."

Dimitri hailed a cab, I provided a quick goodbye and off they went into the distance. Another cab pulled up, me opening the door as my sister piled inside.

"What's going on?" I asked.

"You ruined this trip. You made it all about her."

"What are you talking about?"

"Your mother. You know how I feel about here. Instead of this being about siblings connecting you made it all about her."

"You're only here because of her. How do you think this was paid for?"

"Fuck you! You know our past. I hate that cunt."

"You need to lower your fucking voice." Now I was screaming as loud as Jami.

"Fuck you. You're a fucking drug addict, piece of shit. You live in some shitty, small, shitty, little apartment. You pay too much for. Fuck you, Brian."

"Fuck you."

"You're just mommy's precious."

"I'm sorry you two couldn't get along, but it's not my problem. You're thirty-five, grow the fuck up and get over it already."

"*Fuck you.* Fuck you, you're a selfish asshole."

The cab driver may have been willing to listen to the ranting coming from the two of us, but I sure as hell wasn't. Opening the door, I stumbled out as the cab slowed to take a corner. Nearly falling I gained a footing and jolted over to the sidewalk. It was a two avenue and ten block walk back to my apartment, but it was better than listening to crazy.

The phone in my pocket began to ring.

"Hello?"

"How do I get to my kids?"

"Where are you?"

"I don't fucking know. You left me in the car."

"Are you out of the cab?"

"I don't know where I am."

"What's the street sign on the corner say?"

"I don't know. How the fuck do I get home."

"Look the fuck up and read the fucking sign. *Can you do that?*"

"Fuck you."

Screw it, I'd rather see if Jami makes it back than listen to this shit. But as I ended the call and rounded the corner of Sixty-Second Street there she was. Not alone as when I left her in the cab. Jami had the arm of some random black guy around her shoulder.

"You need to follow me," I said to Jami, walking ahead a few steps before turning back. "You need to go away." It seemed necessary to add this detail.

There wasn't another step in which I looked back until we reached my building. Opening the door, I stood waiting as Jami said goodbye to the stranger who was apparently *so* helpful.

"You fucking left me on the street," Jami screamed, stomping up the stairs.

"Shut the fuck up, people are trying to sleep."

"I don't fucking care. You're a fucking asshole. I fucking hate you, selfish prick."

"You are so out of here."

Jami, still screaming, as we entered the apartment, her kids not looking surprised. As her rant continued I pulled out my laptop and booked three plane tickets back to Salt Lake.

"There. Done. You have three tickets, your plane leaves at six. You need a cab to the airport now."

"No, I'm not fucking going anywhere."

"You can leave, or the cops can make you leave."

"I don't fucking care. Call the cops."

"You got it."

Lifting my phone, the kids started tugging on their mom. I felt bad as I watched them trying to get her off the barstool and out the door. They'd done this a thousand times in at least three states.

"911, what is your emergency?"

"Hi, I have a belligerent drunk in my apartment who is refusing to leave."

"Fuck you. We're leaving. I fucking hate you."

As they opened the door with bags in hand I hung up on the operator. Following them out to the street I hailed a cab, telling the driver where to go and to which airline they needed to be dropped off. Helping my nephew put bags in the trunk I apologized to he and Desiree. This was nowhere near the trip I had planned, but it was a clear reminder why we weren't close and why I moved away so long ago.

Ten minutes later when the door buzzer rang I assumed Jami's mouth had gotten the three tossed from the cab.

"Hello?" I said, holding down the button for a reply.
"NYPD."

Fuck me. Of course they can trace where the call came from. Holding the button down to buzz in the officer I grabbed my keys and bolted down the steps, meeting them on the second floor.

"Hi, I'm the one who called."
"You're trying to remove someone from the apartment?"
"I was, but she finally left. I'm so sorry. I didn't think you guys would be coming."
"As long as everything is alright."
"Everything's fine. Thanks. Again, so sorry you had to come here."

The two beefy lady copies trotted back down the stairs and out the door. I'd not had to call the police since I was twelve and my mother's ex-husband was threatening her with a pair of scissors while my stepsister and I hid in the bedroom. Apparently, nothing in this family will ever change.

19. Connections

Seven consecutive days of berating is what followed Jami's quick departure. Angry text messages informing me of how the meltdown was fueled by my actions. The specific actions not being clear, but whatever the actions were in Jami's head, I certainly was the source.

My reaction to all of this intense drama was to simply ignore it and let the situation evaporate. Jami and I had very different relationships with our mom, and it was clear this would forever plague her, me being the beneficiary of a happy relationship. That's when I made what one could call a mistake. I shared my thoughts in the only way I know how...by blogging. I relayed the story to the web of random followers who give my posts the time of day.

The retelling of the night to end all nights and my opinions as to how and why it all went down only reignited Jami's rage. I wasn't aware she paid any attention to my online ramblings, but she certainly was giving them attention now. The comments she left were intended to be hurtful, though they came across as reactionary and repetitive. Most of what she wrote, in poor grammar, was the same slew of hate spit out in the cab.

It was only when Jami included Desiree in the act of retaliation that I decided to make her comments public. If she so strongly needed to try and knock me down, I would give her the opportunity. It is, of course, only fair that we all have a platform to share our opinions. Even if this particular platform is mine, I'm willing to share for the moment.

It was after this I decided we needed to effectively cut ties. I blocked my family from social accounts, mainly as a way to slow the emotional bleeding. I wouldn't let a stranger speak to me in a way family members now are and it wasn't worth my time to read their angry rants. Phone numbers were then blocked and email accounts filed under junk. It may seem immature on my part, but I find not retaliating as the most effective way to distance myself from the situation. This is a problem I didn't create and I'm in no way capable of repairing. Perhaps one day in the future we can try to connect once more. Though I must admit I have zero interest in mending fences.

With Jami and the kids in the metaphorical rearview mirror, I went back to regular, drama free life. At least, I thought everything would go right back to normal, until I agreed to a date with Gabe. We met on a Friday, spent four hours chatting and realized we had an unusually high number of things in common. Once we came to the discussion of a dislike for small children and laughing at the general masses, I was sold.

Rent (minus) Control

Our first date was one of those perfect first dates you rarely see in real life. We met at my apartment, watched two movies I'm in love with, both of which Gabe could quote until he was blue in the face, and then fooled around. Yes, we had the first date sex.

The sex was good for the most part. My main complaint would be the foreplay. I'm of the generation of guys who like to get in, get off and get out. For someone to spend an hour giving you a blowjob, there's so much time for a mind to wander. And wander it did. While attempting to remain hard I found my thoughts drifting towards work and writing, then remembering I'm being watched, letting out a few fake moans and closing my eyes. It's like being a dog, if I can't see him, maybe he can't see me.

As one hour turned into two and I was miles from climax, I finally brought Gabe to the end. But he gave me a surprise by moving around and popping off on my face. Like a scene right out of a bad comedy, my jaw hung open in shock, white ooze splattered over my nose, lips and chin. Damn I should have shaved because nothing is worse than trying to get cum out of your stubble.

Most guys pass out post orgasm and that was the case for Gabe. This allowed me time to shower, have a glass of wine and eventually crawl back into the bed. At this point I began analyzing my thoughts and feelings about the relative stranger next to me. I was definitely getting the stomach flip and butterfly feeling. A nice change considering the last time I can remember this feeling was when I was twenty and a completely naive.

Even with these positive feelings, the nagging pessimist residing in the forefront of my mind was sharing his bitter opinion. This is going too well, this is moving too fast and I'm not being logical. Ignoring my own thoughts I pushed for sleep, eventually fading away.

The next morning Gabe went home to shower and I headed off to the gym. Our initial meeting and the following date meant no time for exercise on Friday. The gym is my form of therapy. A little running, lifting and music can relax even the highest strung person and bring them back to a pleasant calm. Not long into my workout Gabe sent a text message. *What time do you want to meet?*

I was looking forward to seeing Gabe again, but it was a little soon considering we only departed one another an hour ago. But like a sucker I agreed to meet up later in the evening. What is there to lose?

"What did you think of the movie?" Gabe asked as we exited the 86th Street Cinema.

"I liked it. At the end, maybe you heard, the lady behind me say, *that's it?*"

"No, I missed that."

"What do you mean, *that's it?* The movie had a great ending with actual meaning."

"It's hard when you're expecting a Tyler Perry comedy and then get something philosophical."

"True. There's no hope for the human race," I teased.

Gabe and I had highly compatible senses of humor. Which is nice, usually my friends are the only people to think my remarks are funny. Strangers either find them offensive, racists or oppressive. I think most people are close-minded and boring.

"Let's stop in here for a drink. My friend is bartending and I told him we'd swing by."

Following Gabe, we entered a dimly lit restaurant with a bar near the entrance. Uptown, is the name I think I saw as we passed under the burgundy awning. A twenty-something crowd, mostly straight guys, stroking each other's egos as they guzzled beer, showing each other strange amounts of bro affection.

The dim lights made for the perfect date environment. Red eyes, flushed cheeks and other drunken tells could be concealed as the clear glass bulbs hanging above only allowed enough light to cast shadows on faces. It could also easily turn into a date rape situation as this would be an easy spot to drop something sinister into another person's drink.

"Hey guys, how we doin?" asked a cheerful looking blonde bartender, placing menus on the cherrywood bar.

"Mark, this is Ryan."

"Nice to meet you."

"You too," I replied, grasping the extended hand and returning a firm shake.

"What have you been up to?" Mark asked, leaning forward to reveal a bald spot behind the upturned bangs.

"We saw a movie, thought we'd come in for a drink and wash away the shame of humanity."

"Good decision."

"How's it been in here tonight?" Gabe asked.

"We had a private event earlier, which is why I have these." Marked turned to grab a tray of enormous chocolate cupcakes covered in white frosting and sprinkles. "Take some."

Gabe looked at me. This is one of those gay moments when you don't want to admit you secretly love all the bad foods that taste delicious. I figure I went to the gym today, having one cupcake isn't going to turn me into a whale. Taking one of the decadent demons from the tray, I began pulling down the paper wrapping, curling around the edge.

"How 'bout we split it," suggested Gabe.

Was this his way of telling me not to gorge myself and get fat? Probably not, it's just the gay voice in my head being overly sensitive. While at the same time, the straight voice in my head is saying, *'Don't you dare touch the fucking cupcake or I'll break your fingers.'*

"Sure," I conceded and allowed the splitting of the dessert.

Ten seconds later, cupcake devoured, all I wanted to do was reach over the bar and grab one of the many cupcakes left unattended on the serving tray. Resisting, and not wanting to get tossed out by Gabe's friend, I returned focus to the conversation.

"Have you ever been to a therapist?"

"No." This was an interesting question. "I figure it's not worth paying someone two-hundred dollars an hour to do what my friends do for free."

"Good point. I think I'm the only person to ever have a therapist tell him they don't need to come back."

"What do you mean? Like the therapist wasn't willing to see you?"

"I went to my guy for five years and finally he told me I'm fine and there's really no reason to see him on a regular basis."

"That's a terrible business practice. If he keeps admitting to people they don't need to see him, he's for sure going to go out of business."

Gabe went on to explain how he was in a pristine state of mental health. It was a little on the boring side to listen as someone explained their superiority to the rest of society. I think most people are morons and they make me crazy, but on the flip side I'm as crazy as anyone else.

"I would describe my mental health as being logically insane."

"How does that work?" Gabe asked, sipping at his glass of water.

"Well," I tried to gather my thoughts. It's hard to articulate some things, especially when you don't want to scare the hell out of your date. "I want to think of myself as logical, even more so these days. I try to base my decisions on what's going to serve me best. At the same time, the voices in my head, some of which have not yet grown up, nag at me to do the fun thing, or the erratic thing. It's like being possessed by the devil, except I'm my own devil."

"I've never heard someone refer to the voices in their head as the devil."

"I'm happy to be your first," I laughed, Mark returning with two glasses of wine. "Good timing, this was just beginning to get serious."

"Yeah? What are you ladies talking about?" Mark leaned in, Gabe preparing to answer. "Hold on." Mark trotted off to the center of the bar where a girl with large breasts and a low cut dress was leaning forward to get attention.

"Saved by the drunk," I said, tasting the wine. 'This is good, kinda bitter, but doesn't linger on your tongue."

"Mark knows his wine."

"And I know I like anything in a bottle."

Date two was off to a great start. There was chemistry, he has nice friends, well, the one friend I've met is nice, and the conversation flows. In an effort to break my habits of self-sabotage dating, I was putting effort into resisting the urge to pull away. Maybe this guy is worth the time.

20. Revelations

At some point in life you will say words that seem utterly harmless. To the person you say these words they will be transformative, damaging and problematic. Now I find myself standing outside the restaurant, Uptown, at the end of what began as a good date. Gabe was disputing my views and informing me why my way of thinking is incorrect.

I should back up and explain the verbal error that catapulted us into drama territory. Somewhere around our third or fourth glasses of wine the topic of sex was presented. Sex is not a topic I shy away from, but this wasn't anything dirty, no discussion of preferences or positions. Although there was a question of *'are you a top or bottom,'* which is something every gay man has to ask and answer on a regular basis. No, this sexual discussion was on the meaning of sex.

Gabe believed sex should always have an emotional component. Casual sex wasn't an option as it didn't allow for people to connect. This is a perfectly respectful, wholesome, and to me, conservative view of sex. Which is where the problem comes into play.

I shared my view of sex. Sex and emotion are not tied together in some inseparable fashion. It is possible to have sex for fun, this is the act of casual sex. Most gay men in New York City center their entire lives around the concept of casual sex and there's a booming mobile application industry specifically designed to help guys find dick at the tap of a finger. This is not to say you can't have emotions involved in sex. Of course you can, but I don't think the feelings have to be there for the sex to happen.

Gabe strongly disagrees and dislikes my views. Which is now the new topic of heated debate.

"I'm sorry for pissing you off. That wasn't my intention." I wasn't sorry, but it seemed like the thing to say in an effort to end a futile argument.

"I'm not angry, just disappointed," said Gabe, his height made it possible for him to stare over my head and off into the distance.

"You were upfront about how you think of sex and I thought it was important to be clear right from the beginning how I view sex."

"I'm not sure what to do here."

Never had I been on a second date which devolved into such uncomfortable tension so quickly. Gabe was a nice guy and I did like hanging around him, I'd even venture to guess my friends would like him. Which is why I decided to make a suggestion.

"Maybe we should just be friends instead of pursuing a relationship."

"Really?" Gabe's face twisted, apparently this was the exact wrong thing to say.

"I don't want to never see or hear from you again, but sex is kind of a big deal."

"Maybe you just need to give yourself time to evolve."

"I'm not going to start dating you with the promise of changing. Just like I wouldn't expect that of you. If I did, it would be a blatant lie."

"But if you give it time you might feel differently."

"I might. But are you willing to say you might feel differently about sex in a few weeks or months?" I asked, the question was only fair.

"No."

"Neither am I. So how do you think this is going to turn out?"

Gabe resumed his silent stare into the night somewhere over my head. His visible displeasure was making me uncomfortable. There was nothing I could say that was going to make this better.

"I hate that you did that?"

"Had an opinion?"

"I hate that you jumped right to the friends options," Gabe explained. "It's such a typical gay thing to do. Instead of trying to work through something you just turn away."

"I feel like we're talking in circles at this point."

My ability to be rational was beginning to fade. This was a second date for Christ's sake, all I see in this moment are blaring warning signs that we are not meant to proceed.

"My therapist would say you're emotionally stunted."

With this statement I have officially moved from frustrated to annoyed, verging on angry. When someone begins speaking from their therapist's point of view I want to punch them in the throat. Who gives a shit what your therapist thinks? If you require a person telling you how to feel and then can only parrot their ideas, you don't deserve to have an opinion.

"I'm gonna head home."

"So that's it? We're not going to figure this out?" Gabe looked stunned by my decision to depart.

"There's nothing to figure out. This can't work. You want sex with feelings and I want to date someone who doesn't need sex to be happy."

"Fine, if that's how you feel."

"That's what I think." This isn't about feelings, that's my entire point.

"I guess I'll go home. I'm going to make an appointment to see my therapist on Tuesday."

Just what Gabe needs, someone to tell him the way he *feels* is right and I'm wrong. Clearly, the only reason people go to therapy is for affirmations reflecting their own ideas. I still think the same thing can be achieved with friends and a few bottles of wine.

It wasn't too late and the evening was unusually mild for late summer. Walking home was an opportunity to decompress and burn off some of the alcohol coursing through my veins. Headphones on, I flipped though contacts looking for the one person who would be able to comprehend my frustration: Rachael.

"Hi, panda husband."

"Hey, what's wrong?" I asked, the tone of Rachael's voice was different than normal. It sounded like she may have been crying.

"AJ and I are done."

"Who?" Rachael moved through guys as quickly as I did, so I wasn't entirely sure who she was referencing.

"The guy I've been seeing the past few months off and on. He told me he wants to be with some other girl."

"Then he's not worth your time."

"I know, but this fucking hurts. I hate love."

"Love hates us too."

Rachael sounded worse now than any breakup I could recall. If there is such a thing as soul mates I would say Rachael is mine. We are exactly alike in all except one way. When it comes to love Rachael falls in it easily and hard. Her tough looking exterior conceals one of the most emotionally open and giving people I've ever met. This often causes her pain as men are good at playing with feelings for sex. Coincidentally, this is probably what Gabe's therapist is going to tell him. It's a small world and we're all acting out the same set of stories amongst different groups of people.

If there is a funny or ironic component to our friendship it's that Rachael shares my view on sex not needing to be emotional, but almost always allows her feelings to seep in and cause chaos. Even though she sounded more emotionally distraught than during previous breakups, the story was familiar. She met the guy, fell for the guy, fucked the guy and then he turned out to be a jerk. This being why I profess to Rachael we should not do anything more than sleep with guys we meet in bars. You can never turn a bar guy into dating material. In the end, he can't stay away from the bar and he's always looking for his next fuck.

"What are you doing panda?"

"I was calling to complain about my date, but you've had a rough night so I won't make you listen to my whining."

"Tell me about your date. Maybe it will make me feel better."

I recounted the evening for Rachael, leaving out the extended debate provided by Gabe curbside.

"The funny part of all this is, I thought I was doing the mature thing by being clear about how I think and feel. Usually I would hide or ignore the obvious flaw and let it play out on its own. Maybe it's a sign that I'm just not relationship ready."

"I think it's selfish of this guy to tell you how to feel."

"I mean, I think it's fair for him to have his concept of sex as he does, but he couldn't understand why I wasn't willing to do a three-sixty for him."

"His loss. I wish you were here to drink red beer with me." Rachael loved cheap beer mixed with tomato juice. Not my favorite, but it makes her happy.

"I'd rather you be here. Then we could go play."

"Me too. Everything here is shit. I'm so depressed, I don't even want to breathe."

"The picture you posted on my Facebook page yesterday had me worried. You looked so pale I thought your mom would be calling me today to say you had overdosed on a handful of pills."

"I know, I look and feel like shit. I just can't take enough pills and booze to numb myself better."

"I'm worried about you. I can't get a call telling me you're dead. I need you. You're my other half."

"I know, panda. I'm only holding on for you at this point."

This sentence terrified me. If Rachael was really only continuing to breathe because of me it wasn't helpful to be two thousand miles away. The distance between her and any assortment of pills was only a hand's reach away. It was easy to see between me and the pills, the pills have the unfortunate ability to be a bigger influence.

"Why don't you come stay with me? New city. New life."

"I can't."

"You can. You can either drive out, or we'll get you a plane ticket and you can have a fresh start."

"I have to stay. My DUI hearing is in a month and then there's a trial. It's a bunch of bullshit."

"What about after that?"

"I want to."

This was another circular discussion. I've asked Rachael to come live in New York countless times. Her parents even offered to move her at one point. She may be the only person I have a positive influence on in this life. This is something to which her parents are very much aware. And on a selfish level, I would love to have my best friend in the city and not just on the other end of the phone.

"I need to go to bed, panda."

"No more pills tonight. Promise?"

"Okay."

"Will you call me tomorrow?"

"Yeah, I'll call you on my work break."

"Alright, I love you. Try to feel better."

"Love you too. Bye, panda."

I may not be relationship ready as far as having someone in my life. But I do have friendships in my life that are incredibly important. To know any of my friends is suffering and I'm unable to help makes me insane. Being helpless isn't something I can easily or willingly accept.

21. Bottoms

As the final days of Dimitri's job ticked by and he counted down to the beginning of his new job, we found time for a lunch time walk. Nothing fancy, just coffee and a stroll around the Upper East Side. On one hand I'm happy for Dimitri and his new career opportunity, while on the other I'm sad he'll be working on the other side of the city. Meaning no more midday rendezvous.

"I finally finished your book."

"I didn't realize you were still reading it," I confessed, counting back in my head how many months had passed since I gave the book to Dimitri.

"My friend Rob also recently finished reading it."

"Yeah, he pinged me online and let me know he was reading. Which strokes my ego."

"We were talking about the book and there's something missing."

Not exactly what I was hoping to hear.

"Should I tell you?"

"Um, yes." Was there a discrepancy in the story? Perhaps there was some major typo I'd missed in editing.

"I like the story, but Rob and I both agree there's no lesson at the end to wrap things up."

I've received lots of feedback on my last novel. A few readers gave great reviews on Amazon, others providing less than stellar remarks about my work. One critic going so far as to call the character based on me, 'naive.' I don't dispute the remark as the story is about growing up and into yourself. Maybe it's just not conveyed in the way I hoped.

"You have a point."

"Don't get me wrong, there doesn't have to be, but it feels like maybe there needs to be so it's complete."

"It's something to think about. The story overall is really supposed to be very episodic. I'm sharing a story, but it's stitched together from the fragmented events making up my life."

"Anyway, I just wanted to let you know."

"I appreciate it. It's always good to hear someone else's perspective."

"Do you have any plans tonight?" Dimitri asked, rounding the corner we started heading up Second Avenue and back towards his office.

"There's this kid I've been chatting with a little. He wants to come over and hangout, which of course is code for have sex," I admitted.

It had only been a few days since my Gabe date disaster and I wasn't in the mood for a real date, but it didn't seem there was any harm in a little fun. And it was an opportunity to illustrate my thoughts on sex not having to be emotional.

"I'm being good and staying in tonight."

"That sounds like a terrible Friday night."

"I'm going to see my family on Long Island tomorrow."

"I feel like your mom wouldn't judge you for going with a hangover."

"You're right," Dimitri laughed. "You'll have to report back on this guy after you meet him."

"It's only going to be a hookup."

"Exactly, what do you think you're supposed to report on?"

"Got it. I'll be sure to share back all the dirty details."

"Alright, I have to get back to the office. Text me later if the hookup goes bad."

"Okay, see you later."

Since I'd yet to officially commit to seeing Gio tonight, I sent a quick text. *Want to stop by around 8?* The reply was quick. *Yes.*

Straight guys have it easier than gay guys in my mind. Girls are willing to let you be a little sloppy and still put out. Gay guys on the other hand want you to look perfect. If you don't look perfect then you're just asking them to fuck someone else.

Doing my best to follow the unspoken rules of gay, I made my way home after seeing Dimitri, showered, shaved just about everything there is to shave, had a glass of wine, cleaned up the apartment and put on easy to remove clothing. And it's a good thing I did because twenty minutes before eight the buzzer rang and Gio was at my door.

"You got here fast."

"The train was pulling in when I got to the station."

Gio reminded me a lot of Leo. He had the olive complexion, dark hair and eyes, my usual type. The only difference here is his age. Twenty-five. Usually younger guys turn me off but this kid is too cute to ignore.

"Do you want a glass of wine?" I asked, already pouring Gio a glass.

"I'll sip at it," he said, accepting the glass. "I like your apartment."

"Thanks, I've only been here a few months. I was on Eighty-Fourth before this."

"I like the blue," said Gio, referencing the fresh paint on the living room wall standing between us and the bedroom.

"Do you want to watch a movie?"

"Sure."

Gio followed me to the couch sitting his drink on the coaster I had strategically sat out in advance. It's easier to hide certain obsessive compulsions by doing things before people arrive. Turning on the television I began to scroll through the online selection of movies. Until a hand began running up my thigh, under the leg of my black shorts.

"You don't waste any time."

Gio didn't reply, leaning in and pressing his lips against mine. He's a good kisser, forceful but not sloppy. The stubble of his upper lip scratched at my cheek as he moved from lips to neck. Running a tongue along the curve, Gio pushed me back against the arm of the couch, running a hand up my shirt, the other pulling down the shorts.

Having not put on the obstacle of underwear, Gio's mouth moved from neck, to nipple, to navel and then shaft.

"I thought you said you were a bottom?" I asked, Gio's head bobbing up and down in my lap.

"I am," he said, head coming off the tip, hand still motioning up and down on the shaft.

"You're the most aggressive bottom I've ever met."

With that said, Gio took my hand, leading me into the bedroom. Pulling off his shirt and pants he crawled over me.

"Suck it."

I wasn't in a position to argue. So I did as he asked. The aggressive, forceful attitude was a turn on.

"Lick my balls."

Still honoring the first request, I moved a hand down to feel what I was getting into. The room was dark enough to conceal if there was a mound of hair. It turned out Gio had done as much prep work as me. Balls smooth, I was willing to honor the new request. This continued, me moving back from one request to the other. Until Gio turned me on my stomach. Definitely not a bottom move.

His tongue started at the top of my neck, catching the lobe of an ear. Slowly sliding over the shoulder and all the way down the back. And then he went lower. It was warm, wet and slightly awkward. Being rimmed is not one of my favorite activities. I admit it feels good in this moment, but it's one of the things I would never ask for and refuse to reciprocate. Letting out a gasp, then a moan, Gio stopped.

"Do you want me to fuck you?"

I did actually. But he told me he was a bottom so there was no scenario for the evening where I thought he'd be trying to stick a dick in me.

"I'm not exactly prepared for that," I said, hoping to come off as playfully cute.

"No worries. I understand."

Gio turned me over again, filling his mouth with flesh, his free hand moving in the shadows. Reaching for the nightstand I opened the drawer and located the bottle of lube. Giving us each a squirt things accelerated. Gio on his back, he finished me off and then himself. As he came I felt the warm, wet sensation across my arm and chest.

I chuckled as it happened.

"What?" Gio asked, his voice shaking as though he had made some terrible and embarrassing mistake.

"Nothing," I fibbed. I was laughing because instead of thinking about Gio, I was now wondering if he had gotten cum on my comforter. I hate doing laundry.

22. Dates

"How are you?" Larry asked, sitting next to me at the bar of Ninth Avenue Saloon.

There is no better bar in the city to find cheap drinks and unpretentious gays. It's a little odd this place is able to exist in the heart of Hell's Kitchen. I'm sure it will be pushed out at some point by a new bar, a terrible clothing chain or annoying neighbors who complain about noise.

"Things are pretty good. I feel like I haven't seen you in forever."

"It's been almost two weeks."

"This is what happens when people go on dates. There's no time left to play with friends."

"Truth."

"How is the dating pool treating you?" I asked, sipping at the overwhelmingly strong vodka soda. The bartender was generous with his pour, so patrons must do their best to not have a facial spasms as they drink.

"I've been on a few first dates and one second date."

"Oh la la, a second date."

"I know, right? He's nice but I'm not sure I'm feeling anything. I have been talking to another bottom who lives near me."

"Are you guys going to meet?"

"Yeah, I figure why not. He's cute and we've been talking forever. We can always hangout and if it comes to sex, jerk off together."

"You know, I'm really surprised by the bottoms who won't fool around with other bottoms. It's not like there always has to be a top in the room."

"Unless you ask a top," added Larry.

"That's true. Gotta get those, *masc-musc*, guys who can really pound you. Douche bags."

With a glass clink and a sip through red stirring sticks, we continued.

"What else is going on with you, how'd the whirlwind of dates go?"

Last weekend I had a rush of dates due to bad planning. I'd agreed to four dates on one day. Fortunately, one cancelled, one rescheduled for the day before and the other two were at different times on the same Saturday. This translated into three dates in less than twenty-four hours.

"I definitely don't have the stamina for speed cereal dating," I confessed.

"Did any of them make an impression?"

"The first guy was really nice. Witty, smart. The second guy took me to a play. The play was better than the date, but he's the kind of guy I'd like to become friends, but not date. And the last guy is from Italy. Cute and sweet, but he instantly began talking shit about New York being dirty and awful. That's not the way to get into my pants."

"I hate when people do that."

"Seriously. It drives me crazy. I explained to him there are two types of people who move to New York: Those who get it and those who don't. Those who don't get it just fade away and return to the horrible suburbs from whence they came."

"No second date then?" Larry asked, knowing it was unlikely.

"I'm probably not going to worry about date two or three. I do want to see the first guy again. No plans are set, so we'll see. Gabe sent me a text today, that's still over the top."

"Who is that again?"

"He's the one who was ready to make babies and was planning our future on date number two."

"Right. The crazy one."

"The bad part is he isn't even crazy, he knows what he wants, he just refuses to allow anyone to not want what he wants."

"What did he say in the text?"

"Coyly called me a slut."

"Oh, how sweet of him."

"Asked if I've found any new guys on OkCupid to date, dump and write about."

"Is he hoping to get a starring role in your blog?"

"I'm not sure what the intent is. If he was hoping to convince me of another date, he'd probably not go this route. Or maybe he thinks I like being bullied into submission. Either way, I politely told him no and sent a smiley face."

"Any response?"

"Nope. I assume he got the hint."

"Probably not."

"True. Again though, he makes me like the Leo's of the world even more."

"Yeah, it's easy to get sucked into the emotion free guys."

"I look at the few people I know who are in long-term relationships and don't understand how they get there."

"Me either."

"Especially the few committed gay couples I know."

"I don't think many of them are monogamist," Larry suggested, and rightfully so.

"Probably not, but then I wonder, why be together if you're sleeping with others?"

"There's something to companionship."

"Is it terrible to feel I can get that from you guys?"

"No, but some people just need the other person to feel secure."

"Damn us for being independent. Cue emotionally climactic music."

Could Larry be right, are people pairing off for the sole reason of not wanting to die alone? It's odd to think anyone in New York can feel alone with so many people around at all times, but in a way we're all alone all of the time. Maybe it is worth investing the time in someone, even if you have to share them, just to ensure there's someone to share a conversation.

"Well, if you or Dimitri get married just promise to not vanish."

"What makes you think either of us will ever get married?" Larry asked, finishing his drink.

"Maybe you won't. Maybe you will. But I figure if I put a little pressure on you now, you won't pull the always popular, disappearing act, so many other couples do."

"I guarantee you, we're not going anywhere. Plus, you could always get married."

"The day that happens we are going out to buy lottery tickets."

23. Lessons

Sitting alone in the apartment, laptop glowing in front of me, Dimitri's words from days before swirled inside my head. Lessons. Or lack of lessons. My last book didn't have a lesson. In my head the lesson was life in general. The character based on myself was naive and slightly immature. The lesson there was learning to consider other people and step outside your own mind, even if only for a moment. Perhaps that didn't make any sense to others.

What about in life, not just in my books? Have I learned a lesson? It's easy to say no and profess things are the same as always, but I think I have actually learned something. Other situations are still unfolding to unveil themselves as lessons I hope, or at least turn out to be more meaningful than they currently appear.

The moment the call came to inform me of my mother's death I was jolted. Up to that moment I felt as though I were no more than seventeen. That's the age when I graduated high school, left home and started my adult life. Not the life I was born into, not the life people wanted for me, but my life, the life I wanted to create from the dreams in my head.

Year-after-year I aged, but never felt any older. I graduated from college, wrote like crazy and even managed to produce a few books. Relationships came and went, my cynical and sarcastic side grew and became a major part of my perception of the world. In the midst of all this I still felt seventeen. I was older but still a kid at heart.

Then the news came. The news of something so shocking that there is no way to not hear or acknowledge the information presented. The illusion of seventeen, which encapsulated all aspects of my life, was shattered into so many unrecognizable shards that picking up the pieces meant cutting past the skin and into the soul. The only option was to leave all of the broken on the floor and walk away and into the future.

The future, stemming from the past, is not bleak nor sad. My siblings, who I have officially terminated communication with are spending their energy on anger over the past. Something which confuses me as you can't argue with the dead. And holding a grudge against a dead person is only a personal torment. The future is ours to determine, and that's what I want.

It would be easy to pretend things are the same, go on dating eagerly and only going on first dates. Keep people at arm's-length and never let them in, but what good is it doing? One lesson is to at least let a few people in to some degree. I surely won't become someone new overnight, but it could be worth giving someone, like the guy from my most recent date the opportunity to engage with me before tossing him aside and labeling him as nothing more than a blog entry.

Another lesson I've learned is directly related to who I am. People keep asking me if I'm angry. The question is confusing. Should I be angry? People keep saying I have every right to be angry. Do I? Does anyone have the right to be angry?

My mom picked up a gun, put it in her mouth and then pulled the trigger. Even thinking the thought is uncomfortable, but it's reality...it's what happened. It would be easy to be angry at her and say she was selfish. But that's not fair. I wasn't there and I can't understand what she was feeling physically or emotionally.

Cancer is a terrible disease. It moves fast and eats you alive. If you know you're going to die, no matter what, and you don't want to subject yourself to toxic treatments that can only prolong the inevitable, is it so far-fetched to think anyone might decide to end things on their own terms? I can rationalize and understand the decision. And I can't be angry.

My mother and I had a great time together. She is...was...the most alive person I've had the pleasure of knowing. Even if she hadn't been my mother I'd have been lucky to know her. What I've learned from her is that I can handle difficult situations. Not silly dramatic breakups with guys who are only half interested, but life altering situations. I know I handled things well as Dennis, my friend, and my father both asked me if I would be their decision maker when their day comes.

Rent (minus) Control

With my birthday approaching I have the urge to do something new. It's going to be odd not hearing a familiar voice on the other end of the phone, singing happy birthday in a tone deaf way. Grabbing my phone I sent a text message to Larry, Dimitri and Dennis. *Want to go to Paris in September?* Awaiting the answers I pondered the thought of a trip to Europe. I'd never been, but it would be an opportunity to start a new year of my life in a fresh city with a fresh dose of culture.

The future is bright and mine to design, but I can't allow myself to be limited and stuck in the conceptions of myself created by a past that no longer exists. It's time to take a new leap and start a new chapter. Here goes nothing.

Alternate Ending

23. Lessons

September arrived, bringing my birthday and a trip to Paris. I'd never been outside of the country, unless you count Mexico and Canada. Which I do not. With four friends in tow we boarded a plane, crossed an ocean, and together experienced a new culture.

Paris was incredible to say the least. I'm ready to pack my bags and shack up in a tiny flat just to have more time with this city. The food, the people, the history. There's so much in this one small place. Not to say the entire trip was only tours and wine tastings. Aside from the thirty plus bottles of wine consumed in our flat over the week-long stay, there was plenty of antics.

Brittany, a friend from Baltimore who was sharing a room with me, was up for anything. At one point we put on swimwear and swam in the bathtub. This was no easy task seeing as the tub was about the size of a large bucket. One person could fit at a time, so I sat on the floor taking photos and refilling our wine glasses as we giggled like children.

The trip was life changing as it opened my eyes to an entire world outside of New York that I've been overlooking. That's not to say this New Yorker is ready to abandon his city, but I do want to start seeing the world before it's too late.

And after Paris I had the opportunity to go on a second, third and fourth date with the guy from my twenty-four our dating extravaganza. Not my usual type, Nick, an Italian living way Uptown with his family, worked in the publishing industry. To be clear, when I say way Uptown, I mean in the streets running into the two-hundreds. I wasn't even aware they made it that high. Don't you fall off the edge of the world at some point?

A good guy, Nick didn't fit my usual profile for men. He wasn't Latino, he was a little shorter than myself and skinnier. In fact, he is the exact opposite of nearly everyone I've ever dated or had a sexual encounter. But the personality was amazing and that was the draw.

Things only lasted eight weeks and Nick had his fill of me. Politely dismissing me over the phone while I was on a business trip. Simply stating things weren't going to work and that he felt we should stop seeing one another. Being blindsided, I obliged his request, said goodbye and going about my evening.

Why do I bring this up then if it was so perfectly cut and dry? Well, I took Dimitri's comments on my last novel to heart. What is the lesson? If I'm sharing all of these experiences with the world one would think something is to be learned and gained. This concept paired with the recent events that have changed my reality have made me reconsider some of my behaviors. This is not to say I'm wanting to run off and get married, but maybe a relationship isn't the most terrifying thing in the world.

Nick and I met online, as almost all gay people seem to meet in this manner today. Our dates went well and before I knew it he was spending several nights a week at my apartment. Rather than do my usual dance of pushing away and withholding I went in the complete opposite direction.

Nick was introduced to my friends, I let him know exactly what I thought of pretty much everything, and more or less gave him full access to me as a person. Which is exactly what turned out to be the problem. A few weeks after he sent me back into the dating pool I decided to ask him what his exact reason for doing so was. I was a bit surprised when he actually gave me an answer.

As it so happens, me allowing him to see exactly who I am, the bluntness of my feelings towards everything was a huge problem. It turns out, Nick would have been better served by the illusion of me that is generally served up during a hookup. Knowing the actual me was unappealing and emotionally toxic.

But again, why share all of this detail? No one was hurt in the midst of this mini-breakup. Seeing as we were never officially dating I'm unsure if it even counts as a breakup. I did however gain valuable insight into myself. For years now I've thought I was emotionally dead or damaged. It turns out I'm emotionally slutty.

Somehow I failed to realize that all of my stories and sharing are really just a personal expulsion of feelings. I didn't recognize them as such because usually you only hear from people that they are happy, sad or in love. As if these three states of being define who we are as people. My emotions are so scattered across the spectrum that half the time is just appears to be cynicism or bitterness.

I will say I'm damaged, but in the best way possible. If you can live in a city like New York and not be covered in battle wounds, you're doing something wrong. I've learned something from every one of the guys I've dated or fucked. From the Devil, whom I still have a great distaste for, right up to Nick, who really did nothing but say he wasn't interested. They've each left a mark.

So the lesson is this: People will come and go. Some will pass away and you'll never have another opportunity to say all the things you suddenly need to say. So, while we have the opportunity, have the uncomfortable conversations, ask all the questions you need answers to and live your life in a way that makes you happy. Because once the party is over, it's truly over.

Other Works

The Other Realm

The Other Realm: Blood Vengeance

The Anomaly

Rent (minus) Control

Rent (minus) Control: Turning Thirty

Dust in the Wind

For more information visit: www.rbwinters.com

Synopsis

Ryan is jolted as his former life is brought roaring into the present as death becomes a reality. Returning home to clean up the mess, Ryan does his best to remain stone-faced and emotion free. But can he live through this and be the same person? With each page, Ryan tries using humor to stumble forward and leap past the reality of pain.